Berlitz

Tunisia

- A (☛ in the text denotes a highly recommended sight
- A complete A–Z of practical information starts on p.104
- Extensive mapping on cover flaps and throughout the text

Berlitz Publishing Company, Inc.

Princeton   Mexico City   Dublin   Eschborn   Singapore

Copyright © 1995 by Berlitz Publishing Co. Inc.
400 Alexander Park, Princeton, NJ, 08540 USA
9-13 Grosvenor St., London, W1X 9FB UK

All rights reserved. No part of this book may be reproduced or trans-
mitted in any form or by any means, electronic or mechanical, including photocopying, recording or by any information storage or
retrieval system without permission in writing from the publisher.

Berlitz Trademark Reg. U.S. Patent Office and other countries
Marca Registrada

Original Text:	Neil Wilson
Photography:	Chris Coe
Editors:	Alan Tucker, Stephen Brewer
Layout:	Media Content Marketing, Inc.
Cartography:	Visual Image

*Although we make every effort to ensure the accuracy of all infor-
mation in this book, changes do occur. If you find an error in this
guide, please let our editors know by writing to us at Berlitz Publishing Company, 400 Alexander Park, Princeton, NJ 08540-6306.
A postcard will do.*

ISBN 2-8315-7332-7
Revised 1998 – Second Printing February 1999

Printed in Switzerland
029/902 RP

CONTENTS

What to Do 80

TUNISIA

TUNISIA AND THE TUNISIANS

T unisia is the smallest country in North Africa. It reaches a mere 200 km (125 miles) from the palm-fringed sands of its Mediterranean beaches to the sand-fringed palms clustered at its desert oases. Within its borders, however, there is a rich and varied culture waiting to be discovered.

A strategic location and fertile farmland have made Tunisia a much-coveted territory, captured and defended repeatedly through the ages by successive waves of invaders. The Phoenicians, Romans, Byzantines, Arabs, and Ottomans left a legacy of ruined temples, forbidding fortresses, magnificent mosaics, and ornate architecture for historically minded travellers to explore. No less alluring are the exotic sights and sounds of the present-day country: the crowded *souks* of Tunis, crammed with colourful goods and redolent with the rich scents of leather, spices, and cedar-wood; the hoarse bellow of a camel at the Thursday market in Douz, and the yammer of Arabic as flowing-robed nomads haggle over its price; the nimble fingers of a Djerban potter shaping an elegant urn from the pink island clay; and the gap-toothed grin of an elderly fisherman mending his nets beneath the kasbah walls in the old port at Bizerte. All these and more lie within easy reach of the popular holiday resorts lining the Mediterranean coast.

Squeezed between its giant neighbours, Libya and Algeria, Tunisia runs only 750 km (465 miles) north to south, and at most 350 km (217 miles) east to west. Its winding coastline is 1,200 km (744 miles) long, however, and has some of the finest beaches in the Mediterranean, while the varied landscapes of the interior range from the oak forests of the northern hills to the sand dunes of the Sahara Desert.

The ornate doors of Tunisian buildings make coming and going a colourful experience.

The northern part of the country is dominated by the fertile plain of the Medjerda Valley, which was once known as "The Granary of Rome," and which is still the source of Tunisia's wheat harvest. To the north of the Medjerda are the thickly wooded chains of the Kroumirie and Mogod mountains, where forests of pine and cork oak overlook the attractive, rocky north coast, renowned for its pink coral reefs and remote, sandy beaches.

South of the valley is the Dorsale, an east–west range of hills that runs into the Cap Bon peninsula and divides the wetter north from the semi-arid steppe of central Tunisia. The central coast is known as the Sahel, where the famous beach resorts of Sousse and Monastir bask beside the warm, shallow waters of the Gulf of Hammamet. Inland, the holy city of Kairouan and the Roman amphitheatre of El Djem bake in the dusty heat of the plains.

The huge salt lake of the Chott el Djérid almost cuts the country in two, and marks the northern edge of the desert. To the south are the shifting sands of the Grand Erg Oriental, a vast sea of dunes that extends far into the Sahara. Off the south coast lies the "desert island" of Djerba, the "Land of the Lotus Eaters" described by Herodotus and Homer, which is now a paradise for sun-worshipping tourists.

The population of Tunisia is around 8½ million, and concentrated in the north, especially around Tunis and Sousse. The people themselves are a mixture of Berber and Arab blood, but through the centuries the Berbers have been thoroughly assimilated into the dominant Arab culture. Only 2 percent of the population is now identifiably Berber, and the Berber language has all but died out, though traces of their former way of life survive in the *ksar* villages of the south.

Classical Arabic, the language of the Koran, dates back to the seventh century.

In the Saharan oases you will see black tribesmen descended from the original Sudanese slaves who were transported to Tunisia by Arab slave traders, a practice which did not die out completely until the middle of the 19th century.

The victorious Arabs of the seventh century brought with them the religion of Mohammed, and while the Berbers resisted at first, Tunisia was eventually united under the banner of Islam. Like all Muslims, Tunisians must adhere to the principles known as "The Five Pillars of Islam." These are: to accept

Storefronts are often completely covered with samples of the wares on sale inside.

The exquisite Tunisian beaches attract millions of sun-seeking visitors each year.

that "There is no God but God, and Mohammed is his Prophet;" to pray five times daily, at dawn, midday, afternoon, sunset, and after dark; to give alms to the poor and towards the maintenance of the mosques; to fast between sunrise and sunset throughout the month of Ramadan; and to attempt to make the pilgrimage to Mecca at least once during their lifetime.

Tunisians are friendly, and proud of their country and its history. In the country areas in particular, you will often find yourself the recipient of real, old-fashioned hospitality: you will be offered tea, and asked about your travels, your home, and your family. Great pleasure will be taken in answering your own questions about the village, its history, and traditions.

Too many tourists miss out on the best of Tunisia by sticking to the package-holiday resorts of Hammamet, Monastir, and Djerba. Make the effort to explore a little farther afield, and you will discover something of the true Tunisia that lies beyond the beaches.

A BRIEF HISTORY

Tunisia as a nation-state is a creation of the 20th century. This small country, strategically situated at the crossroads of the Mediterranean, has a long and complex history stretching back far into prehistory.

Primitive tools and weapons found near Gafsa in southern Tunisia have been dated to 6000 B.C. and are attributed to nomadic hunters called the Capsian culture. These people probably migrated from western Asia, perhaps as long as 10,000 years ago, and it was their descendants who were encountered during the second millennium B.C. by the first Phoenician traders who ventured along the North African coast.

Contemporary accounts describe them as light-skinned and speaking an unintelligible language. The Greeks called them *barbaros*, meaning "not of our people" or "uncivilized," and this persisted through the ages as "Berber." (The English word "barbarian" comes from the same root.)

Phoenician Pioneers

The Phoenicians were the first permanent settlers on the Tunisian coast, and they established trading posts at Sousse, Utica, and Bizerte (12th century B.C.), prior to founding the city of Carthage in 814 B.C. (just north of present-day Tunis). Being brilliant navigators and traders, they spread throughout the Mediterranean world from their home cities of Tyre and

Carthagenian ruins: an ancient sanctuary, possibly used for human sacrifices in the Phonecian era.

Sidon on the Levantine coast (in what is now the Lebanon), and soon became masters of the seas.

Although it was the Phoenicians who invented the cursive form of writing on which all subsequent European alphabets were based, they left no written record of their achievements. Most of what we know about them comes from Greek and Roman accounts, which often include rumours of the Carthaginian custom of child sacrifice. Hundreds of funerary stones have been uncovered in the ruins of ancient Carthage, but controversy continues in academic circles as to their origins.

> The Arabic language is written from right to left, though numbers are written left to right.

Dynastic rivalries in Tyre and Sidon allowed Carthage to gain more power, and when the Levantine cities fell to Cyrus the Great of Persia during the sixth century B.C., Carthage became the undisputed centre of Punic (Phoenician) civilization. From North Africa to southern Spain, and the eastern Mediterranean to the Atlantic, Punic settlements were established. Carthaginian captains took command of the Strait of Sicily, and challenged the Greeks for control of the trade routes.

The Rise of Rome

Meanwhile, the fledgling Roman Republic had increased in strength to the point where it threatened to gain control of the strategic islands of Corsica and Sicily. The struggle for supremacy between Rome and Carthage led to the start of the First Punic War (264–241 B.C.).

This was primarily a naval campaign. Before one of the many sea battles, the Roman admiral Claudius Pulcher consulted the sacred fowl which were kept aboard his flagship, hoping for a positive omen. The chickens were supposed to peck at their grain if he was to win, but they ignored the corn

HISTORICAL LANDMARKS

c.1200 B.C. Phoenicians establish trading posts along the North African coast.

814 B.C. Phoenicians found the city of Carthage.

264–241 B.C. First Punic War between Rome and Carthage.

218–201 B.C. Second Punic War; Hannibal crosses the Alps.

146 B.C. Third Punic War ends with the sack of Carthage.

44 B.C.–2nd century A.D. Romans rebuild Carthage; the city flourishes.

A.D. 439 Carthage falls to Vandal invasion.

671 Oqba ibn Nafi founds holy city of Kairouan at the time of the Arab Conquest.

800–909 Aghlabid Dynasty and Tunisia's "Golden Age." Building of the Great Mosque of Kairouan.

1159 The Almohads take Tunis.

1535 Barbarossa captures Tunis for the Turks.

1574 Tunisia becomes part of the Ottoman Empire.

1837–1855 Reign of Ahmed Bey, Tunisia's first ruler open to Western influence.

1881 Tunisia is made a French protectorate.

1934 Habib Bourguiba founds the Neo-Destour Party.

1942–1943 Tunisia is the scene of fierce fighting: the Allies quash Rommel's desert campaign.

1956 Tunisia is granted full independence.

1957 Tunisia declared a republic; Habib Bourguiba is the country's president.

1987 Bourguiba replaced by Zine el-Abidine ben Ali.

1989 First free elections since 1956. Zine el-Abidine ben Ali elected president without opposition. His party, Democratic Constitutional Assembly Party, wins landslide victory.

1990s Islamic fundamentalism gains foothold, resulting in crackdown on all Muslim militants.

1994 Ben Ali reelected without opposition.

The people living in mountain villages of the Tunisian south continue to follow their ancestral traditions.

scattered on the deck. Claudius, a notorious hothead, tossed the sacred birds overboard to the applause of his crew, and charged into battle. He lost his entire fleet.

Rome may have lost that battle, but they did in fact win the war, having built a new fleet based on the design of a captured Carthaginian warship. Carthage was forced to pay huge war reparations, but the humiliating defeat rankled with such a proud people, and it wasn't long before they invaded Spain, prompting Rome to declare the start of the Second Punic War (218–201 B.C.). It was this war which saw one of the most famous military campaigns in history.

Since Rome controlled the sea, the Carthaginians, led by a general named Hannibal, had little choice but to attack over-land. Hannibal set out on his famous expedition from his Spanish beachhead at Sagunto, crossed the Alps with more than 30,000 men and around thirty elephants, and eventually clashed with the Roman army in 216 B.C. The battle, at Can-nae in southern Italy, was a devastating blow for the Ro-mans, who suffered losses of over 50,000 men. They were not denied victory, though, for the Roman general Scipio fi-nally crushed the Carthaginians on their home ground at Zama, forcing them to burn their fleet and surrender all terri-tory except a small corner of eastern Tunisia.

Carthage continued to trade, and grew rich again, exciting the jealousy of Roman merchants. The Third Punic War (149–146 B.C.) saw the Romans besiege the city of Carthage for two years. When it finally fell to Scipio in 146 B.C., the original population of around a quarter of a million people had been reduced to 50,000. The city was razed, the sur-vivors sold into slavery, and the land ploughed with salt so that nothing would grow from the ruins. The proud Cartha-ginian Empire had been obliterated, and its territory was subsequently absorbed into the Roman province of Africa.

Only 100 years later, Julius Caesar decreed that the blight-ed city should be rebuilt, so by the second century A.D. Carthage had become a flourishing Roman centre of 300,000 inhabitants, complete with temples, forum, triumphal arches, theatres, baths, and, after some time, churches. The city also enjoyed access to the fertile hinterland of northern Tunisia in the Medjerda Valley.

Tunisia was under Roman rule for about 600 years in all, until barbarian hordes swept through Europe and into North Africa in the fifth century A.D. By the year 439, an army of Germanic tribesmen, the Vandals, had occupied the province, pillaging Roman cities, smashing statues, and laying waste to the countryside. Their leader, Genseric, was known as "lord" of Carthage. When he died, the country collapsed in anarchy, allowing the Byzantine army of Emperor Justinian to take over in 534 A.D.

Arab Conquest

United under the banner of Islam, Arab armies poured out of their homeland during the seventh century, and within a hundred years had created an empire which encompassed lands from Persia, through Egypt and North Africa, into Spain and part of France.

Of the early Arab generals, none was bolder than Oqba ibn Nafi, who conquered the Maghreb (Arabic for "the west"), a region which today includes Tunisia, Algeria, and Morocco. His army reached Tunisia in 670 A.D., travelling inland to avoid Byzantine strongholds along the coast. Ignoring the infidel city of Carthage, he established his own capital at Kairouan, saying "I shall build a town to be a citadel of Islam for all time." From this base, he set off to the west, subduing all in his path until he reached the Atlantic coast of Morocco, calling on God to witness that only the ocean could prevent him going further.

The Arab Empire, which had begun as a simple religious community ruled by the Prophet Mohammed, was now a vast and far-flung kingdom. Dozens of different peoples speaking scores of languages lived within the Arab dominions and held tight to their ancient traditions. The Berbers, inhabitants of the lands north of the Sahara since prehistoric times, did not feel inclined to submit to Arab rule without a fight, and many tribes opposed the occupation.

Shortly after Oqba's invasion, a nomadic Berber tribe made a counter-thrust, led by an influential queen known as El Kahina (The Prophetess). Her forces recaptured much ter-

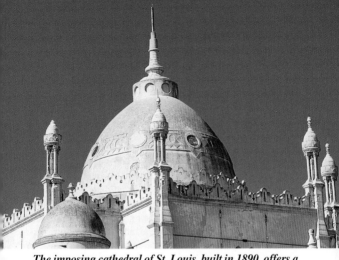
The imposing cathedral of St. Louis, built in 1890, offers a good view of Carthage and the Bay of Tunis.

ritory, and it took the Arabs five years to put down the revolt. After a final confrontation in the amphitheatre of El Djem, El Kahina was executed and her head sent on a platter to the caliph in Damascus.

Tunisia lay a long way from Damascus, however, and the local rulers, influenced by both the recalcitrant Berbers and the radical Islamic scholars of Kairouan, developed a strong independent streak. In 797 A.D., the caliph appointed a provincial leader, Ibrahim ibn Aghlab, as governor of Tunis. Ibrahim declared himself *emir* (prince), and he and his descendants ruled Tunisia for more than a century, until ousted in 909.

The Aghlabid era is generally looked upon as Tunisia's "Golden Age." The city of Tunis, which had been developed as an Arab port a century earlier, was expanded, and the Zitouna Mosque was erected, along with the Great Mosques of Kairouan, Sfax, and Sousse, and the *ribats* (fortified monasteries) at Sousse and Monastir. Trade and agriculture flourished, and successful military campaigns captured Malta, Sicily, and Sardinia, and even went as far as sacking St. Peter's in Rome in 846 A.D.

The Aghlabids were succeeded by the Fatimids, who conquered Egypt and moved their capital to Cairo. Tunisia slipped into anarchy, overrun by the hostile nomadic Arabs of the Beni Hilal tribe. Disorder and mayhem were quashed with the arrival of the Almohads, the fundamentalist rulers of Morocco, who captured Tunis in 1159, and who at their height ruled an empire stretching from their capital of Marrakech to Libya and Spain. They held Tunisia for 70 years, implementing an orderly government, religious discipline, and a renewed prosperity. It wasn't to last, though, for the unity of their empire gave way when the local governors in Tunisia founded their own dynasty, the Hafsids, who ruled from 1228 to 1574.

With Tunis as their capital, the Hafsids fast grew in power and splendour. The city's first *médersas* (religious schools) and the picturesque souks of the perfumers (Souk Attarine) and cloth merchants (Souk des Etoffes) are just a small part of their architectural legacy. The great Sultan Abu Abdullah al-Mustansir (1249–1277) assumed the title of *caliph,* and was acknowledged by Mecca as the Commander of the Faithful. In 1270 a crusade was undertaken against al-Mustansir, with France's heroic King Louis IX at the head of the army; but the crusade ended in failure, and Louis died in Tunis.

Turkish Domination

Khayr ad-Din—better known as Barbarossa (Redbeard)—was a Turkish corsair from the Aegean island of Lesbos. With his brother Aruj and their pirate fleet they terrorised

Spanish and Portuguese shipping from their base on the Tunisian island of Djerba. Barbarossa had grander ambitions, however, wanting an African dominion for himself. To this end he submitted to the Ottoman sultan in Istanbul in return for military support. He captured Algiers in 1529, was made admiral of the Turkish fleet soon after, and then went on to take Tunis in 1535, defeating the Hafsids. Thus by 1574, Tunisia had become part of the Ottoman Empire.

With the arrival of the Turks, Tunis became a medieval sea power. The corsairs, who were especially active in the Christian slave trade, became the terror of all shipping that was not Ottoman. During the 17th and 18th centuries Tunisian pirates made their country rich and powerful, and they were soon operating independently of the Turkish sultan. The bey of Tunis, who had originally been appointed every three years by the sultan, began to pass on his title by heredity. By the late 1700s, the Turkish beys had been so deeply absorbed into Tunisian culture that they were in fact Tunisian in everything but name.

Inhabitants of southern Tunis continue to wear their traditional clothing, in spite of the heat.

Under Ahmed Bey (1837–1855), the country made its first significant move to detach itself from a medieval society and join the developing world. Slavery was abolished and European aid was sought to build a modern army. New banks, factories, and communications were set up, but Europe was already too far ahead. The pirate ships of the Barbary Coast were driven from the seas by swifter and better-armed European steamships, and the European powers began looking towards North Africa for new territories to conquer for their growing empires.

Towards Independence

France had already seized Algeria in 1830, and so now set its sights on Tunisia. On the rather flimsy pretext that Tunisian tribesmen had made a raid into Algeria, the French occupied Tunis and declared the country a protectorate. Under the Treaty of Bardo, signed on 12 May 1881, the bey was recognised as nominal ruler, but all the power was in the hands of the French.

The colonial experience was a disastrous one for the majority of rural Tunisians who were displaced from their land by French and Italian immigrants. The professional classes still managed to live comfortably, however: they learned to speak French, sent their children to study in France, and adopted many French customs. Despite being articulate and well-educated, though, the upper reaches of the administration were closed to them. The inevitable frustration prompted by this urban élite resulted in the birth of the country's first nationalist movement.

First came the Young Tunisians, a group of intellectuals modelled on the Young Turks, who began agitating for the overthrow of the Ottoman sultan in Istanbul. They gained little popular support, however, until a bloody uprising in 1911 was cruelly suppressed by the French. The "Jellaz Affair" stirred nationalist feeling among all levels of Tunisian society.

In 1920, the Destour Party was formed (*destour* meaning "constitution" in Arabic); its objective was to work with the French towards greater Tunisian autonomy, but it ended in inertia and failure. A new shot of spirit was needed.

In 1927, a young Tunisian of exceptional ability arrived back in Tunis, with his new French wife, having studied law in Paris. Habib Bourguiba sympathized with the Destour Party at first, but soon he came to believe that there could be no progress without struggle, and forcefully expressed his views through newspaper articles. In 1934, he founded the Neo-Destour Party, which set out to gain massive popular support for self-determination. In that same year he was arrested, accused

Pirates of the Barbary Coast

The Muslim corsairs roving the seas along the Barbary Coast (the North African coast from Libya to Morocco, named for the indigenous Berbers) were financed by wealthy backers in Tunis and Algiers in return for a percentage of their booty. The privateers attracted mercenaries from all over Europe, and their ships, called *galliots*, were powered by oars and were faster, less conspicuous, and more manoeuvrable than contemporary sailing ships. A pirate *galliot* would race up to a merchantman or a coastal town, attack, take hostages and booty, and speed away again. Strict discipline was enforced at sea, and any man who was slack in his duties was summarily executed. When the pirates returned in triumph to Tunis, the whole town would explode with feasting and debauchery. Every man of the crew would be rich—even the galley-slaves who pulled the oars—once he had sold his portion of the loot. The merchants of Tunis bought all the stolen goods and later disposed of them at a good profit. Christian prisoners were sold into slavery, bringing good prices if they were craftsmen or had other special skills. Any nobles or wealthy merchants who were captured were quickly ransomed.

The father of modern Tunisia rests in the mausoleum of the Bourguiba Mosque, in Monastir.

of being a political agitator, and sent to jail for three years. His continued activism led the French to dissolve the party in 1938, and Bourguiba and his colleagues were interned in France.

When the Allies, headed by General Eisenhower, landed in North Africa towards the end of 1942, the Germans and Italians seized Tunisia as a vital base for the desert campaign being waged by Rommel. The area became the scene of fierce fighting for five months, until Commonwealth and American forces triumphed over German troops in May 1943.

By 1945, prospects for negotiations resulting in major concessions from France did not seem good, and Bourguiba left Tunisia to set up a Committee for the Liberation of the Maghreb in Cairo. By 1948, he had become president of the Neo-Destour Party and a noted public figure, travelling extensively to campaign for Tunisian independence. Realising that they would have to negotiate with Bourguiba, the French invited him to Paris for talks, at which concessions were obtained and promises of increased autonomy were given. The promises were not implemented, however, and groups of armed patriots began resorting to more militant tactics. When Bourguiba returned to his country, he was again arrested and thrown into jail.

Bourguiba's arrest inflamed already swollen passions, and bloody clashes became more frequent. A fierce resistance to the idea of concessions from Paris grew among the French settlers in the country, but in 1954 Pierre Mendès-France, the French premier, publicly recognized Tunisia's right to self-government. The following year a new French premier, Edgar Fauré, met officially and publicly with Bourguiba to sign a protocol granting Tunisia internal autonomy. Habib Bourguiba came back to Tunis in triumph, and on 20 March 1956, Tunisia gained full independence (although France retained their military base at Bizerte until 1963).

Tunisia Today

The country was still nominally ruled by the bey up until 25 July 1957, when Tunisia was declared a republic with Bourguiba as its first president. The sweeping social reforms which he was responsible for included advances in education, the emancipation of women, legal restructuring, and attempts at secularisation. His popularity was such that he was overwhelmingly reelected to three further

Indigenous date palms are the main source of income on many Tunisian oases.

terms as president, and in 1975 the National Assembly named him president-for-life.

His future was not so easy though, for economic troubles and increasing Islamic fundamentalism in the late 1970s and early 1980s led to widespread unrest, and in November 1987, at the age of 84, Bourguiba was forced to relinquish power due to old age and ill health.

Bourguiba's influence was felt in every corner of Tunisian life, and he is still fondly regarded as the father of modern Tunisia. (It is hardly surprising that every town and city now has its Avenue Habib Bourguiba.) A magnificent mausoleum and memorial mosque have been erected in his hometown of Monastir.

Tunisia today is regarded by the West as the most moderate and liberal of Arab states, and despite its small size it plays an important role in international affairs. Tunis hosted the Arab League from 1979 to 1990, and the city has been the home of the Palestine Liberation Organisation's headquarters since 1982. The country also maintains close ties with both France and the U.S.A., and has important trade links with western Europe generally. Perhaps more than anything else, its highly successful tourist industry has made it the most widely known Arab country among Europeans.

Bourguiba's legacy is a tolerant and forward-looking nation which enjoys one of the highest standards of living in the developing world. Tunisia is a small but vigorous country, of which its people are justifiably proud.

A Tunisian Glossary

The following are common Arabic and Berber words:

aïn	spring	killim	woven carpet with geometric design
bab	entrance, gate		
bordj	fort		
chott	salt lake	ksar	fortified village
dar	house	maqroudh	semolina sweet-meats made with syrup and date paste
jemâa	mosque		
jebba,	long-sleeved		
jellaba	tunic		
djébel	mountain	médersa	religious school
erg	region of sand dunes	médina	old town
		mergoum	embroidered mat
ghorfa	fortified stone house	ribat	fortified monastery
hadj	pilgrimage (to Mecca)	souk	market street
		tophet	place of sacrifice
kalaâ	fortress	zaouïa	house of a religious order
kasba	citadel; fortified part of médina	zerbia	knotted carpet

WHERE TO GO

Tunisia is a compact country, and many interesting places lie within an easy day trip from the coastal resorts. One of the most popular excursions is to the cosmopolitan capital city of Tunis, and the nearby ruins of ancient Carthage.

 TUNIS

Tunis is actually three cities in one. To start with, there's the modern capital of the Tunisian Republic, a city of tree-lined boulevards, modern buildings, and bustling sidewalk cafés, which has a distinctly European flavour. Then, there's the medieval Arab *medina* (old town), an exotic maze of narrow, angled streets lined with tiny shops, grand mosques, and impressive palaces. Lastly, there's historic Carthage, the ancient Punic capital, where crumbling ruins are surrounded by flower-bedecked suburban villas.

You can easily spend two full days exploring Tunis and its surroundings, although a day and a half will be sufficient if you're rather short of time.

The backbone of modern Tunis is the broad boulevard of **Avenue Habib Bourguiba,** stretching between the medina and the Lake of Tunis. Here, along the shady central promenade, kiosks piled with newspapers, magazines, and books alternate with fragrant flower stalls, while offices, sophisticated cafés and luxury hotels line the pavements. (Following the deposition of Bourguiba in 1987, the street was officially renamed Avenue 7 Novembre, but even today everyone still refers to it by its old name.)

At the western end of the avenue, the place de l'Indépendence is dominated by the façade of the Catholic **cathedral** of St. Vincent de Paul (1882), a legacy of French colonialism. Facing it from the opposite side of the square is the

Tunisian Highlights

Tunis Medina. The historic heart of Tunisia's capital is a labyrinth of narrow streets and shady souks: admire the Islamic architecture of historic buildings, or haggle for carpets and other local wares with good-natured shop-keepers. (See p.28)

Bardo Museum. *Boulevard 20 Mars, Tunis.* The national archaeological museum houses a superb collection of Roman mosaics and other priceless artefacts. Bus no. 3 from Av. Bourguiba, or Metro Line 4. Open 9am–5pm (summer), 9:30am to 4:30pm (winter), closed Monday and public holidays. Admission charged, plus additional fee for camera or video. (See p.34)

Sidi Bou Saïd. A village perched above the sea to the north of Tunis. Spend an afternoon souvenir hunting, then visit the neo-Andalucian house and music museum, Ennejma Ezzahra. (See p.39)

Dougga. Originally the Roman city of Thugga, now the best-preserved Roman ruins in Tunisia. Be sure to see the Capitoline Temple, the Baths of Licinius, the House of the Trefoil, and the intriguing Mausoleum of Ateban. Open 8am–6pm. Admission charged, plus additional fee for camera or video. (See p.40)

El Djem. This magnificently preserved Roman amphitheatre dating from the third century A.D. seats 30,000 people. Open 8am–6pm. Admission charged, plus additional fee for camera or video. (See p.59)

Chott el Djérid. Mirages shimmer above the desolate beauty of the Sahara's (and North Africa's) biggest salt lake. Oasis towns Tozeur and Nefta offer respite in the shade of the palms; the sand dunes of Douz, a good base for excursions into the desert to the south, mark the "Gateway to the Sahara." (See p.70)

Matmata. Tunisia's renowned "troglodyte" village, with underground houses carved out of the soft earth. If you can, spend a night in one of the village's subterranean hotels. (See p.75)

Ksar Villages. The settlements of Chenini, Douiret, Guermessa, and Ksar Haddada, with their cave dwellings and fortified communal granaries (*ksar*), were the last Berber strongholds. Now they are among the most scenic villages in the country. (See p.76)

French Embassy. Here the boulevard narrows to arcade-lined avenue de France, which leads to the gates of the medina.

☛ The Medina (Old Town)

The medina of Tunis is probably the most hassle-free medina in all of North Africa, and certainly the easiest to navigate. At all the main gates you'll find a large map with all the streets clearly named, and there are small orange signposts pointing the way to the principal sights. The souks are refreshingly free of the hustlers who have become the bane of tourists in Marrakech, Fès, and Cairo; the only place you might be collared by a tout is at the carpet-sellers souk.

The free-standing archway of the **Bab el Bahr**—also called the **Porte de France** (built 1848)—marks the entrance to the medina. It was once continuous with the thick medina walls,

Habib-Bourguiba street—a lively avenue, animated and verdant—in the heart of the modern city.

and stood on the shore of the Lake of Tunis (the Arabic name translates "Sea Gate") before the French built their new town on reclaimed land. To the right of the gate is the British Embassy, housed in a picturesque Moorish building straight out of the *Arabian Nights*. Walk through the Porte de France and then take the left-hand of the two narrow alleys facing you.

This is the **rue Jemaa ez Zitouna**, the medina's main street, and it is lined with tiny crafts shops and souvenir stalls. As you merge with the crowds that shuffle slowly uphill, you will find yourself immersed in a world of heady sensations. Fragrant incense and exotic perfumes compete with the mouth-watering smell of roasting mutton and the aroma of freshly ground coffee. The tap-tap-tap of silversmiths' hammers and the scuff of sandalled feet on smooth paving stones almost drown out the muezzin's call to prayer from a minaret. The bright reds, blues, and golds of flowing caftans flash in the dappled interplay of sunshine and shade, and then the street disappears into a dark tunnel to emerge at the steps below the door to the Zitouna Mosque.

The focus of daily life in the medina for over one thousand years has been the **Jemaa ez Zitouna** (Mosque of the Olive Tree). Founded in 732 on the site of a temple to Athena, the mosque has been enlarged and restored many times; the outer wall used stone taken from the ruins of Carthage. Visitors are allowed to climb the stairs to an arcade facing the central courtyard. From here, you can appreciate the tranquillity of the mosque, a stark contrast to the bustle of the streets outside. The prayer hall is to the left, through a horseshoe arch crowned with a white dome. The square minaret is a 19th-century addition.

The most interesting sections of the medina are clustered around the walls of the mosque. Centuries ago, these narrow streets were roofed over to provide quarters for the city's

craftsmen. Members of high-class guilds such as the book-sellers, jewellers, and perfumers had the best locations, close to the mosque, whereas the noisier tradesmen, such as the metalworkers and saddlers, were housed some distance away so as not to disturb the scholars studying within. The unfortunate tanners, with their noxious smells, were banished even farther afield to the far side of the city walls. Modern times, and the proliferation of souvenir shops catering to the tourist trade, have brought a breakdown of this strict segregation. A few of the old souks (market streets) are still dominated by a single trade, but it's more usual to see a variety of different shops in each souk.

The Bab el Bahr, or Porte de France, marks the entrance to the picturesque labyrinth of the Tunisian medina.

When you come out of the mosque, turn left and left again into the **Souk el Attarine** (Perfumers' souk), which is situated along the north wall. Only a few genuine scent-makers remain, for their expensive creations have been displaced by cheaper modern toiletries. The little shops are stacked with hundreds of tiny bottles filled with priceless essential oils—rose, jasmine, sandalwood, lily of the valley, lavender, orange-flower, vanilla, cinnamon, and clove—and extracts of civet, musk, ambergris, and castor. You can choose a ready-made scent, or have one blended to suit your

> While haggling, do take time to accept the cup of coffee or tea offered to you by the salesman.

fancy. The unusual, many-branched candles hanging in the perfumers' shops are carried at the head of the procession that leads a Tunisian bride to her new home.

First left off Souk el Attarine, running along the west wall of the Zitouna, is one of the quietest souks, called the **Souk des Etoffes** (Drapers). Colourful cascades of cloth, caftans, and blankets muffle the spirited haggling of the shopkeepers. Souk des Etoffes ends at a crossroads at the southwest corner of the mosque. On the right, a warren of tiny streets and alleys crowded with gold- and silversmiths' shops is the **Souk des Orfèvres.** The ringing of hammers issues from a dozen doorways, and shop windows glitter and shine with gold, coral, pearls, and a host of precious stones.

Left is the **Souk de la Laine** (Wool Market), crowded with tailors and weavers working on their hand looms.

The Perfumer's Art

The art of scent-making was regarded by the Arabs as the noblest of trades, and in every city the perfumers' souk (Souk el Attarine) was given the place of honour nearest to the mosque (attar is Arabic for "perfume"). Perfumery is a highly skilled profession and the Tunis scent makers' reputation was the best.

A fine perfume may contain over 100 ingredients, blended in precise proportions—the recipes of famous scents were, and still are, jealously guarded secrets. The raw materials include essential oils extracted from flowers, fruits, and spices—jasmine, lavender, lemon, nutmeg; aromatic woods like sandalwood; and animal secretions such as ambergris (from sperm whales), musk (from musk deer), and castor (from the beaver). The scent maker strives to create a perfume that complements the natural scent of the wearer.

One of the many pieces of ancient art on view at the Bardo Museum.

Straight ahead is the **Souk des Femmes** (Women's souk), which offers jewellers on the right and carpet- and rug-makers on the left. Continue along this thoroughfare for about ten minutes into the southern reaches of the medina to find the **Dar ben Abdallah** (follow the small orange signs on the walls). This 18th-century palace houses the city's **Museum of Folklore and Popular Arts.** The magnificently decorated central courtyard is flanked by four rooms which are home to tableaux of 19th-century Tunisian life, including men having tea, a bride preparing for her wedding, women sewing, and a grandmother teaching young girls about baby care.

Return to the Souk el Attarine beside the Zitouna Mosque, and a right turn onto rue Sidi Ben Arous will bring you to the unmistakable pink marble façade of the **Mosque and Tomb of Hammoûda Pacha** (built in 1655). The story behind this colourful building reveals a bit of Tunisian history. When Turkish governors came to Tunis on the orders of the Ottoman sultan, they brought with them a slightly different form of Islam than that commonly adhered to in Tunisia. The Tunisians lived according to the Malikite rite, while the Turkish conquerors observed the Hanifite. Aware of this dif-

Museums and Mosques

Zitouna Mosque. *Rue Jemaa ez Zitouna, Medina, Tunis.* A legacy of the Hafsid dynasty dating from the ninth century. Open Saturday to Thursday 8am–noon. Admission charged. (See p.29)

Dar Ben Abdallah. *Rue Dar Ben Abdallah, Medina, Tunis.* Museum of Folklore housed in an 18th-century palace. Open 9:30am–4:30pm, closed Sunday. Admission fee. (See p.32)

Bardo Museum. *Boulevard 20 Mars, Tunis.* National archaeological museum: objects from Carthaginian times to the Islamic period. Bus no. 3 from Av. Bourguiba, or Metro Line 4. Open 9:30am–4:30pm (winter), closed Monday and public holidays. Admission charged, plus additional fee. (See p.34)

Carthage Museum. *Take the TGM train to Carthage-Dermech or Carthage-Hannibal stations.* An archaeological museum displaying items found in the ruins of Carthage. Open 8am–7pm (summer), 8:30am–5:30pm (winter). Admission charged, plus additional fee for camera or video. (See p.36)

Sousse Ribat. Late eighth-century fortified monastery: offers a grand view from the top of the lookout tower. Open 9am–noon and 2–5:30pm (summer), 2–5:30pm (winter). Admission charged, plus additional fee for camera or video. (See p.53)

Sousse Archaeological Museum. Excellent collection of Roman mosaics in the medieval kasbah. Open 8am–noon and 3–7pm (summer), 9am–noon and 2–6pm (winter). Admission charged, plus additional fee for camera or video. (See p.54)

Monastir Ribat. A small Museum of Islamic Art housed in a ninth-century fortified monastery. Open 9am–noon and 2:30–6pm (summer), 2–5:30pm (winter). Admission charged, plus additional fee for camera or video. (See p.54)

Great Mosque of Kairouan. A ninth-century mosque located on the site of the oldest place of worship in North Africa. Open 8am–2:30pm and 4:30–6:30pm Sunday to Thursday and Friday 8am–noon (summer), 3–4:30pm (winter). Admission charged, plus additional fee for camera or video (including all monuments in Kairouan). (See p.57)

The famous Bardo Museum, where most of Tunisia's great archeological treasures are kept.

ference, Hammoûda Pacha decided to gave his mosque a Turkish-style octagonal minaret with a gallery, rather than the square type common to the Maghreb, so that all would know that his mosque was of the Hanifite rite.

☞ The Bardo

The Bardo National Museum can be found in a 19th-century Beylical Palace in the western suburbs of Tunis. It is home to many of Tunisia's greatest archaeological treasures, and includes relics from every period of the country's rich history, from Carthaginian times to the Islamic period. Among the exhibits are artefacts which may have been related to Punic rituals of child sacrifice rumoured to have been carried out at Carthage, Roman statuary, and a fine baptismal font from the early days of Christianity. The museum's main attraction is its superb collection of Roman mosaics on the first and second floors. These colourful images provide a fascinating record of daily life in Roman times, with scenes of farming, hunting, and fishing, as well as grander themes depicting mythological events and tributes to the gods. The mosaics range in age from the second century B.C. to the seventh century A.D., and come from all over Tunisia, with some fine examples from Sousse, Dougga, and El Djem.

The most famous image is in Room XV, showing the poet Virgil flanked by two Muses—Clio, Muse of History, on the left, and Melpomene, Muse of Tragedy, holding a mask on the right. Among the other outstanding items are Perseus rescuing Andromeda from a sea monster, and an enormous fourth-century A.D. floor mosaic, which illustrates 23 types of boats, with their names, floating on a sea full of fish. Finally, don't miss the depiction of Ulysses, in which the hero is tied to the mast of his ship to prevent him from answering the Sirens' song, on his way to the island of the nymph, Calypso. His crew row on with their ears plugged.

Carthage

"Carthage" means "New Town" in the Phoenician language, and when the city was founded in 814 B.C., that's just what it was—a new city in a new land. Now, of course, it is the oldest city in Tunisia—at least, what little remains. Sacked by the Romans in 146 B.C., but later rebuilt, this once-great city fell into ruin following the founding of Tunis by the Arabs in the eighth century.

The ruins of Carthage lie 18 km (11 miles) northeast of Tunis city centre, and are surrounded by an upscale suburb of villas and gardens. The site can be easily reached on the T.G.M. electric train, which runs frequently between Tunis and Carthage (see TRANSPORT on page 124). The ruins are

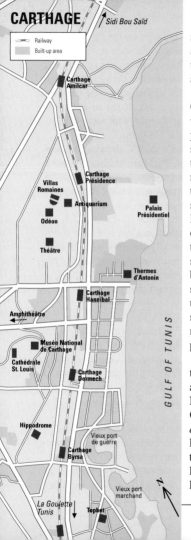

CARTHAGE

→ Sidi Bou Saïd

Railway
Built-up area

Carthage
Amilcar

Carthage
Présidence

Villas
Romaines

Antiquarium

Odéon

Palais
Présidentiel

Théâtre

Thermes
d'Antonin

Carthage
Hannibal

Amphithéâtre

Musée National
de Carthage

Cathédrale
St. Louis

Carthage
Dermech

GULF OF TUNIS

Hippodrome

Vieux port
de guerre

Carthage
Byrsa

Vieux port
marchand

N

La Goulette
Tunis ↓

Tophet

spread out over quite a large area, and to see them all will take the best part of the day, and involve a lot of walking.

If you leave the train at Carthage-Salammbo, a short walk from the station brings you to the **tophet** (place of sacrifice), where for centuries the Carthaginians are rumoured to have sacrificed thousands of their first-born sons to the gods Tanit and Baal Hammon. One school of thought holds that after the unfortunate victims were strangled, their bones were burned on an altar, and the sacrificial remains buried in urns marked by engraved stone slabs called *stelae*, many of which are on display in the Bardo Museum.

The ancient city was centred on the Hill of Byrsa, on a site now occupied by the **National Museum of Carthage** (*Musée National de Carthage*). It is most easily reached by getting off the train at either the Carthage-Dermech or the Carthage-Hannibal station, then walking to the top of the hill. The exhibits include Roman sarcophagi, amphorae, Phoenician stelae, and both Greek and Roman statuary. Many other pieces lie in the adjacent gardens, set in the cypress, pine, and eucalyptus trees. Beside the museum is an excavation which reveals the walls and foundations of Punic houses five or six stories

> **Arabic is a semitic language, and is different in structure from European languages.**

high, complete with water cisterns and drainage channels lined with pink stucco. Next door is the **Acropolium,** a cultural center that was formerly the cathedral of St. Louis.

A number of other ruins lie in the vicinity of the Carthage-Dermech, Carthage-Hannibal, and Carthage-Présidence stations, including the impressive **Baths of Antoninus Pius** (*Thermes d'Antonin*). Dating from the second century A.D., these were among the largest in the Roman Empire, covering an area of 3½ hectares (9 acres). Only the foundations remain of this immense pleasure palace with hundreds of rooms: *frigidaria* (cool rooms),

---

Dido and Aeneas

Legend has it that the city of Carthage was founded by Dido, the sister of Pygmalion, king of Tyre. When her brother murdered her husband for his money, she fled with her followers to North Africa. There, a local chieftain called Iarbus agreed to sell her as much land as could be covered with the hide of a bull. The cunning Dido cut the hide into thin slivers which, when tied together, encircled the Hill of Byrsa. Here, she raised the foundations of Carthage.

The poet Virgil allowed Dido to fall in love with his hero, Aeneas, when he arrived in Carthage after the fall of Troy (even though he would have had to have been 500 years old to have done so!). When, at Jupiter's command, Aeneas abandoned Dido to found Rome, she committed suicide.

37

tepidaria (warm rooms), and *caldaria* (steam rooms); rooms with pools and fountains, mosaics and frescoes; rooms for dining and massage; rooms for worship and exercise — this was the social club and leisure centre of a rich commercial city. A diagram chiselled into a slab of marble on a small observation platform explains the various sections of the baths.

A short walk uphill from the baths leads to the **Roman Villas** (*Villas Romaines*), a group of ruins including the *odeon* and numerous hillside villas. One restored villa houses a small museum, giving a hint of what life was like here in ancient times. Much remains the same as then — the panorama of gentle green hills and vivid blue sea, a praying mantis motionless on a leaf, lizards clambering over the rocks. (One obvious addition to the scene is the heavily guarded modern villa which you can see down below, and which is the Presidential Palace.)

A souvenir shop typical of those on the very narrow streets in the coastal city of Sidi Bou Said.

Downhill from the *odeon*, the **Roman Theatre** is almost entirely a 20th-century restoration. Evening performances of music and drama are staged here during the Carthage International Festival (see page 89).

Sidi Bou Saïd

The picture-postcard village of Sidi Bou Saïd tumbles down a steep slope between its hilltop lighthouse and the sea in a cascade of sugar-cube houses with blue-painted doors and shutters. The village is famous for its unspoiled beauty, for the panoramic view from the top of the hill (go all the way up to the lighthouse), and for the ornate bird cages made by local craftsmen from an arabesque of wire and wood. The cages mimic the shapes of the distinctive wrought-iron window-grills that adorn the houses.

The village is named after the mosque and tomb of a 13th-century holy man. About a hundred years ago it became an exclusive retreat for well-off locals and ex-patriates, and remains so to this day, though its peaceful cobbled streets are invaded daily by coach trips.

To experience the village at its best—in the evening and early morning—you will have to stay overnight at one of the fine local hotels. There are two famous cafés—the **Café des Nattes** and the **Café Chaabane,** both of which offer marvellous views of the village and the sea.

EXCURSIONS FROM TUNIS

Two major Roman sites are within easy reach of Tunis.

Thuburbo Majus

This Roman town, about 60 km (37 miles) south of Tunis, acquired its distinctly un-Roman name from the Berber settlement which predated it. The ruins are spread across an undulating plain, and are frequented by local coin sellers and "guides" who pester you to buy (invariably fake) goods. The centrepiece of the ruins is the **Capitoline Temple,** dating from A.D. 169–192, the majestic columns of which overlook the square expanse of the Forum. The temple was once home to a massive statue of Jupiter, whose head and foot are on display in the Bardo Museum (see page 34). From the temple steps you can see the rest of the site—the row of columns ahead and to the right marks the **Palaestra of the Petronii,** an exercise area adjacent to the Summer Baths. To its left are the **Winter Baths,** with a fine portico and columns of coloured marble from Chemtou in northwestern Tunisia.

☞ ## Dougga

The Roman city of Thugga (today called Dougga), lying 100 km (62 miles) southwest of Tunis, is one of the biggest and best-preserved of all the Roman sites in Africa. Enthusiasts will find enough to keep them occupied for a full day—there is a hotel at the nearby town of Tebboursouk if you want to stay overnight. If you have only an hour or two to spare, then head for the main attractions listed below.

Dougga was a thriving town for several hundred years before the arrival of the Romans in the second century A.D., but it was under them that it grew and prospered. The car park is right beside the impressively complete **Theatre,** with seats for 3,500 and elegant Corinthian columns overlooking the raised stage. The road beyond leads to the splendid portico of the **Capitoline Temple,** which overlooks the **Square of the Winds,** so named because the paving is carved with a compass rose recording the names of the twelve winds.

Downhill from the Capitol is the sprawling ruin of the **Baths of Licinius,** which have a well-preserved central hall, bathing pools, service tunnels, and a hypocaust (under-floor heating) system. Below the baths, a narrow road (note the ruts which have been worn by cart wheels) winds down to the **House of**

the Trefoil. This delicately christened building, with its central courtyard lined with small booths and a trefoil-shaped dining room, was actually a brothel. Next door is the **Cyclops Baths,** notable for a semi-circular latrine in a fine state of preservation.

Right at the foot of the hill is the oddest and most mysterious of Dougga's monuments. The **Mausoleum of Ateban** is a Libyco-Punic structure of the third century B.C., a unique blend of Libyan, Egyptian, Persian, and Greek architectural styles, and one of the few surviving pre-Roman monuments to be found in Tunisia.

Dougga, a fascinating city, is the site of the best-preserved Roman ruins in North Africa.

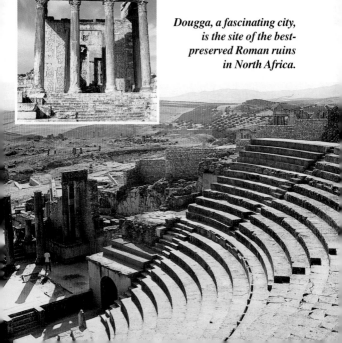

Full of character, the Vieux Port area of Bizerte is the city's most charming neighborhood.

THE NORTH COAST

The northern coast of Tunisia lies at the narrowest part of the Mediterranean—Sicily is only 140 km (87 miles) away to the east. The main sea route from East to West passes through this strait, and the region's history has been shaped by seafarers since the earliest times. A good road leads north from Tunis towards the port of Bizerte, 70 km (43 miles) distant. About halfway, a minor turning on the right leads to the ruins of Utica.

The Phoenicians passed frequently along this coast, and **Utica** was established around 1100 B.C. as a staging post, situated roughly halfway between their home port of Tyre and their entrepôt at Cadiz. The sea once came right to Utica's doorstep, but through the centuries the silt deposited by the nearby Medjerda River has left the ruined city stranded 10 km (6 miles) inland. A museum preserves the relics found in its Punic tombs, and interesting remains of

Roman villas and streets near the museum inspire visions of Utica in its heyday.

Bizerte

You enter Bizerte across a lifting bridge which spans a canal cut during the 1890s to link the sheltered saltwater Lac de Bizerte with the Mediterranean. The first channel here was dug by the Phoenicians, allowing access to this fine natural harbour, which has been used successively by first the Romans, then the Byzantines, Arabs, Turks, and finally the French. Because of its strategic importance, it has been much fought over in the two thousand years since it was constructed, most recently in the 1960s. Following Tunisian independence in 1956, the French continued to occupy their military base at Bizerte until a showdown with Tunisian forces in 1961, when over 1,300 local people lost their lives.

After the French eventually withdrew in 1963, Bizerte was transformed from a busy military and naval port to an industrial port and tourist town, modern in most respects but still retaining vestiges of its fascinating past. Today the **Vieux Port** (Old Port) is the city's most alluring quarter — a tranquil harbour filled with brightly-painted fishing boats and lined by white-washed medina houses. The harbour entrance is guarded by the massive **kasbah** on one side, and the smaller **Fort el Hani** on the other. The latter houses a small Oceanographic Museum and has a pleasant café on the roof.

The hilltop **Fort d'Espagne** (Spanish Fort) above the town is a legacy of Bizerte's pirate past, when the Turkish corsairs would frustrate their pursuers by taking cover within its impregnable walls. At the head of the port, the octagonal minaret of the **Great Mosque** is another echo of the Turkish past.

Stretching north from the entrance to the Old Port is the **Corniche,** a long, narrow ribbon of golden sand lined with reliable hotels and worthwhile seafood restaurants.

At the tip of the long, sandy peninsula to the east of Bizerte, **Ghar el Melh** is another 17th-century pirate port, complete with a number of Turkish fortresses and mosques. The journey to the nearby *koubba* (dome) of **Sidi Aalu el Mekki** passes alongside a fine beach, and there's yet another beautiful strip of sand at **Raf-Raf.**

The Coral Coast

West of Bizerte the main road keeps well inland, while the coast is wild, beautiful, and almost untouched—a series of sandy beaches separated by rocky headlands, backed by thick scrub and forests of oak, eucalyptus, and juniper. The few villages located here once earned a living from the offshore coral, which has been harvested by divers for centuries. The coral is now an endangered species, though, and diving is restricted.

The roads to **Cap Serrat** are not very good, but the swimming, fishing, and snorkelling are excellent. Farther west at **Sidi Mechrig,** the beach is overlooked by the ruins of a Roman bathhouse, and at **Cap Negro** you can see the remains of a French coral-fishing station dating from the 16th century. If you carry on along the Bizerte–Tabarka highway, the mining town of **Sedjenane** is known for its unusual, primitive pottery—intriguing little statuettes in maroon and black glaze. Islam forbids the creation of any sort of human representation, but the craftsmen and women here refuse to end a pagan Berber tradition which is over one thousand years old.

Tabarka

The little port of Tabarka, protected by its offshore island, is a sleepy town for much of the year. Founded by the Phoenicians in 800 B.C., it was originally a trading post, and its harbour was later used by the Romans for exporting the exotic red and yellow Numidian marble, which was quarried at Chemtou, 90 km (56 miles) to the south. In the 16th century it was frequented by the pirate Barbarossa (see page 18), who bought the freedom of fellow buccaneer, Dragut, by handing over the Isle of Tabarka to Charles V of Spain. Charles in turn gave it to a Genoese family, who were responsible for the fort which now crowns its highest point.

The single main street, predictably called avenue Bourguiba, leads to a promenade next to the causeway, which now connects the island to the town. The promenade runs as far as a picturesque rock formation called **Les Aiguilles** (The Needles), a series of curiously eroded sandstone pinnacles and fins. Uphill from the main square is **La Basilique** (The Basilica), a Roman cistern which was converted to a church in the 19th century, and which is now home to a small, interesting museum.

Cork and Coral

The cork in your bottle of Tunisian wine began life as the bark of a tree—the cork oak (*Quercus suber*), which is native to the western Mediterranean, and which grows in abundance in the hills around Aïn Draham, south of Tabarka. The cork is harvested by prising off the thick, spongy bark around the trunk of the tree; the bark eventually grows back, and can be harvested again in approximately eight to ten years.

Traditionally the most popular souvenir in Tabarka has always been jewellery made from the precious coral which grows in the warm seas off northern Tunisia. Its colour can be yellow, purple, or red, but most sought after is the rose-pink variety for which Tunisia is famous. Coral has been gathered from these waters for centuries for use in the jewellery trade, to the extent that it is now an endangered species.

45

In summer, the town attracts large numbers of tourists who come to enjoy the fine beach, the wooded hills, and the excellent scuba-diving. A new complex called **El Montazah,** with hotels, apartments and an airport, has been built at the east end of the beach, roughly 4 km (2½ miles) from the town, and now threatens to shatter the tranquillity of this historic backwater. In addition, a yacht marina complete with holiday apartments, shops, restaurants, and a diving club has been built next to the harbour.

Roughly 50 km (31 miles) offshore lies the minute volcanic archipelago of **La Galite**—home to a colony of Mediterranean monk seals, an endangered species. The islands are a nature reserve, and closed to the general public.

The countryside in the area around Tabarka is covered in lush forests of pine, eucalyptus, and cork oak; it is a landscape that feels more European than African. Roughly 24 km (15 miles) to the south lies the quaint hill resort of **Aïn Draham,** where the white houses with their red tile roofs look equally European, having been built by the French in an attempt to re-

The Aiguilles, "needles" of sandstone sculpted by erosion.

create the atmosphere of an Alpine village. The town is popular with both foreign and Tunisian tourists, who come here for the combination of cool mountain air, bracing forest walks, and nearby hot springs.

Even farther to the south (60 km/37 miles from Tabarka), the ruins of the Roman city of **Bulla Regia** are well worth visiting. Here you have the opportunity to explore a collection of unique **underground villas,** many with superb *in situ* mosaic floors that constitute some of the best Roman mosaics to be seen outside the Bardo Museum.

Once a bustling Phonecian trading post, Tabarka's harbour is now very quiet.

CAP BON PENINSULA

The Cap Bon peninsula is a blunt thumb of land protruding into the Mediterranean, separating the Gulf of Tunis to the north from the Gulf of Hammamet to the south. It is a fertile region of farms, vineyards, and citrus groves, and is home to some of the most popular beach resorts in Tunisia.

Hammamet

The stretch of golden sand between Hammamet and Nabeul is one of the most beautiful in the country, with warm, shallow turquoise water and a lush green backdrop of palms, jasmine bushes, and orange trees. Hammamet, at the southern end, was a quiet fishing village until it was "discovered" in the 1920s by a Romanian millionaire, George Sebastian, who started the ball rolling when he built himself a luxury villa near the beach. Hammamet is now a famous international resort, with over 60 hotels strung out along the shore. Fortunately, development has been sensitive to the surroundings, and the coast has escaped the tidal wave of concrete that blighted the Costa del Sol in the 1960s and 1970s —here the hotels are discreetly set back from the beach, and few have roofs that are higher than the level of the palms. The original mansion built by Sebastian has since been turned into Hammamet's **International Cultural Centre,** where plays, concerts, lectures, and exhibitions are held during the summer months.

These pots probably come from Nabeul, the ceramic-craft capital of the Cap Bon region.

The town itself is clean and pretty, with an attractive shopping centre, and white houses neatly arrayed along the well-swept streets. Various restaurants, shops, and cafés provide diversion for casual strollers. At the southern end, next to the beach, is the tiny **medina,** with the high walls of the **kasbah** in its northwest corner. It was garrisoned originally by Muslim soldiers, and later by the French Foreign Legion, and good views of the town

It is possible to explore the lovely beaches of Hammamet, an internationally-renowned resort, on the back of a camel.

and beach are available from its ramparts. Nestling in its protective shadow are the narrow alleyways of the compact medina, where you can browse among the souvenir shops, and perhaps find your way down to the old Sea Gate.

Nabeul

Nabeul may be the administrative capital of the Cap Bon region, but it is really known as the **pottery** capital of Tunisia. Hundreds of workshops produce a wide range of glazed and unglazed ware, from functional pots and bowls to fancy ornamental vases. Especially striking are the panels of coloured **ceramic tiles,** a Nabeul speciality. The designs are usually traditional, handed down by Andalusian refugees who arrived here from Spain in the 17th century, and include stylized flowers or cypress trees surrounded by a patterned border, all in bold blues, greens, and yellows.

A stroll through the streets reveals other crafts, including **stone carving,** gold and silver **embroidery,** and **perfumes** made from the local citrus and jasmine blossoms. Be sure to visit the fixed-price **Artisanat** (handicraft shop) to see the range and quality of local products before you indulge in any haggling at the market. Although the **camel market** may try to exploit tourists with its souvenirs and camel rides, it offers an insight into Tunisian life, with anything from livestock to local produce for sale.

Around the Cape

Many interesting places are situated within easy reach of the beach resorts at Nabeul and Hammamet. A good road leads north to the end of the peninsula, and back down its west coast, taking in most of the places of note.

The beautiful beaches continue north to the town of **Kélibia,** where the fishing harbour is dominated by an impressive fortress; there are fine views from the top of the sixth-century Byzantine ramparts. Stop here for a seafood lunch by the harbour, or at the rocky coves of Mansoura to the north, and try a glass of the local white wine, which is called *Muscat Sec de Kélibia*, and which is light, refreshing, and medium dry.

The remains of the fifth-century B.C. Punic town at **Kerkouane** are generally regarded as the best preserved of any Carthaginian settlement. The houses are famous for their neat little hip-baths, lined in pink stucco inlaid with white marble chips. The village of **El Haouaria,** right at the tip of the peninsula, has the twin attractions of a bat-filled cavern and a falconry centre. Nearby **Sidi Daoud** offers the spectacle of the *Matanza*, the annual tuna harvest, when local fishermen trap the migrating tuna in huge nets which

Many-coloured fishing boats are still docked along the beaches of Hammamet.

stretch out from the shore. It takes place between May and July, in a ceremony that dates back hundreds of years.

A stunning coast road winds down the hills to **Korbous,** which has been famous since Roman times for its baths and hot springs. A number of hotels and spas are crammed into a narrow ravine beside the sea, where you can take a thermal cure, or just drink your health with a glass or two of the sulphurous mineral waters.

THE SAHEL

The central coast of Tunisia is known as the Sahel (Arabic for "coast" or "margin"), and centres on the cities of Sousse and Monastir. The region attracts thousands of tourists annually to its fine beaches, good hotels, and historic sites, and even the surrounding countryside—an alluring patchwork of fields of grain, olive groves, and wandering flocks of sheep—is an attraction in its own right. The area is also known for crafts, and the inhabitants of the scattered villages are spe-

Only the courtyard of the Great Mosque in Sousse is accessible to non-Muslim visitors.

cialists in embroidery, jewellery-making, and cloth. Two sites are within easy reach of the coast: the holy city of Kairouan, and the magnificent Roman amphitheatre at El Djem.

Sousse

The capital of the Sahel is Sousse, Tunisia's third-largest city after Tunis and Sfax. Although it's a major port and a busy commercial and industrial centre, the workings of the city don't impinge on the relaxed atmosphere of the medina or waterfront. The golden sands stretch for miles north of town, lined with resorts, to the marina of Port el Kantaoui.

Held successively by the Carthaginians, Romans, Vandals, and Byzantines, the city finally succumbed to the redoubtable Oqba ibn Nafi, the seventh-century Arab conqueror of the Maghreb (see page 16). The citizens resisted his siege for two months, but when Sousse eventually fell, Oqba's forces plundered it all the more savagely. Almost all trace of earlier civilisation was wiped out, so that today Sousse boasts a fine collection of Islamic monuments, but few Roman and Punic remains.

Avenue Habib Bourguiba, the main boulevard, stretches from the beach to place Farhat Hached next to the medina, lined by shops, cafés, offices, hotels, and cinemas.

Just inside the entrance to the medina is the ninth-century **Great Mosque** (open 9:00 A.M. to 1:00 P.M. except Friday). From the outside, the mosque looks like a fortress, with round corner towers and crenellated battlements. Inside, the courtyard is paved with bright marble and surrounded by a harmonious arcade; the double pillars on the far side mark the main entrance to the prayer hall (entry is forbidden to non-Muslims, but open doors afford quite a good view). You may notice that there is no minaret—the muezzin used to call the faithful to prayer from the tower of the neighbouring *ribat*.

The **ribat** is an eighth-century fortified monastery, which was once home to a medieval community of devout Muslim warriors who observed a knightly code of conduct—rather like an Islamic equivalent of the Christian Knights Templar of the Crusades. Piety and bravery became their watchwords, and they were valiant in their attempts to be as zealous in battle as they were humble in prayer. An arched gate gives access to the courtyard, lined with cells where the warriors slept. Stairs on the south wall lead to the small prayer hall, and the claustrophobic spiral staircase which climbs to the top of the lookout tower. The **panorama** from here is well worth the climb. You can look down into the courtyard of the Great Mosque, and across the medina rooftops to the massive walls of the kasbah.

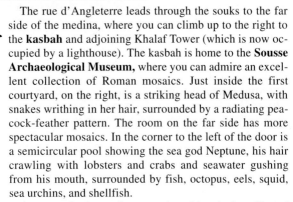

The rue d'Angleterre leads through the souks to the far side of the medina, where you can climb up to the right to the **kasbah** and adjoining Khalaf Tower (which is now occupied by a lighthouse). The kasbah is home to the **Sousse Archaeological Museum,** where you can admire an excellent collection of Roman mosaics. Just inside the first courtyard, on the right, is a striking head of Medusa, with snakes writhing in her hair, surrounded by a radiating peacock-feather pattern. The room on the far side has more spectacular mosaics. In the corner to the left of the door is a semicircular pool showing the sea god Neptune, his hair crawling with lobsters and crabs and seawater gushing from his mouth, surrounded by fish, octopus, eels, squid, sea urchins, and shellfish.

A passage leads to a flower garden with a shady trellis and several fragments of sculpture. The rooms here contain some of the museum's finest mosaics, including a dining room floor (obviously commissioned by a Roman with a sense of humour) decorated with discarded lobster claws, chicken bones, shells, fruit stalks, and fish bones. Another dining room floor shows four gladiators and a host of wild beasts, plus gladiators fighting with leopards (the inscription tells us that the gladiators were awarded a prize of 5,000 *denarii* for their skill by the citizen Magerius). Dining room mosaics can be recognised by their T-shaped outline—tables were arranged around three sides of the "upright," allowing slaves to serve food from the central "aisle."

Monastir

The town of Monastir has a long history similar to that of Sousse, and retains its ninth-century *ribat* and Great Mosque. Unlike Sousse, though, Monastir has been overwhelmed by the tourist trade, and consequently feels more like a new town than an historic port. It is a pleasant resort with a sheltered beach, a marina, and several beachfront hotels right in the middle of town.

The imposing **ribat,** dating from the ninth century, dominates both the harbour and the town. Additions and renovations over the centuries have created a complex of crenellated walls and turrets, with open courtyards and spartan cells. The former prayer hall is home to a small Museum of Islamic Art, which offers displays of woodwork, embroidery, glassware, and calligraphy. The airy summit of the *nador*, or lookout tower, offers a panoramic view over the town. Next to the *ribat* is the plain but venerable **Great Mosque,** built in the ninth to 11th centuries.

The Great Mosque of Kairouan, the most famous monument in the city, looks much like a fortress.

Among Tunisians, Monastir is best known as the birthplace of Habib Bourguiba, the man who won independence for his country in 1956 (see page 23). The **Bourguiba Mosque,** at the edge of the medina, was erected in the family's honour and, though far from ancient (it was built in 1963), its harmonious design and rich decoration help to make it a place to admire. Features and styles have been borrowed from all periods of Tunisian architecture. Go round to the entrance at the

The sacred mosque of Barbier, in Kairouan, is famous for the beauty of its tile decoration.

base of the minaret, and peek at the courtyard through the iron-grilled windows. An imposing avenue leads from the park outside the *ribat* to the **Bourguiba Mausoleum,** an ornate building capped with a gilt dome, and framed by twin gold-topped minarets.

☞ Kairouan

The holy city of Kairouan is the most important Islamic site in all North Africa. This was the place chosen in 670 by

Oqba ibn Nafi to be the base for the Arab conquest of the Maghreb, where he vowed to build "a citadel of Islam for all time." During the ninth century, Tunisia's "Golden Age" (see page 17), the Aghlabid Dynasty made Kairouan the capital of the entire Maghreb. The city evolved into one of the great commercial, religious, and intellectual centres of Islam, but it was sacked by the Beni Hilal in 1057. It is still revered as one the holiest cities of Islam, and referred to as "the city of 50 mosques." (The name Kairouan actually means "caravan," as in a camping place for camel caravans.)

Kairouan lies about 60 km (37 miles) from the coast, in the middle of a semi-arid plain which is given over to olive trees and sheep. There is a new tourist information office on place du Mohammed el Befaouri, located opposite the Continental Hotel and next to the **Aghlabid Pools.** These immense circular cisterns, filled with limpid water, are ninth-century reservoirs, built by the Aghlabid governors. They are fed by a 35-km- (22-mile-) long aqueduct from the hills to the west.

If you continue along the main road from the Aghlabid Pools, you will come to the **Zaouïa of Sidi Sahab,** which is also called the **Mosque of the Barber,** and which is famous for its handsome decorative tiles. Sidi Sahab was a companion of the Prophet Mohammed, so his final resting place is a sacred site and a place of pilgrimage.

The street across the highway from the Aghlabid Pools leads towards the medina; turn left after the kasbah walls and walk for five minutes to reach the Great Mosque. The city's most famous and venerable building, the **Great Mosque** looks more like a fortress with its high walls and strong, easily defended gates. The first mosque on this site was built by Oqba ibn Nafi in 671; the Great Mosque in its present form dates from the ninth century. Visitors are allowed to inspect the **courtyard,** paved in marble and surrounded by a colonnade, and, through open doors, admire the gleaming tiles of the *mihrab* (prayer niche) and the rich marble and porphyry columns in the prayer room, which non-Muslims may not enter. In the courtyard, look for the seven wellheads, their edges worn and notched from a thousand years of hauling bucket ropes. The stocky, square **minaret** is the oldest in North Africa; notice how the lower courses of masonry consist of stone salvaged from Roman ruins. Take a stroll around the mosque after your visit to the courtyard, avoiding the carpet sellers if you can. The **Bab Lalla Rihana,** in the far wall, is the prettiest of the many portals.

The city walls beyond the kasbah lead to Bab et Tounes (Gate of Tunis), the main entrance to Kairouan's **medina.** The main street through the centre of town is lined with souks festooned with Kairouan **carpets,** which are renowned throughout Tunisia for their special patterns and colours. Every second doorway allows snatched glimpses of women making the carpets on primitive looms, while street-corner stalls are piled up with gaily coloured skeins of wool—the carpet-weavers' raw material.

Lying right in the heart of the medina is the **Bir Barouta** (Well of Barouta), concealed within a small, inconspicuous building near the souks. The water is lifted from the well by a mechanism which is driven by a blindfolded camel, which tramps all day in endless circles. This "one-camel-power" pump has been in operation for almost three centuries.

When visiting any mosque, take off your shoes before you enter.

It would be impossible—not to mention a shame—to leave Kairouan without sampling at least one of the local sweets called **maqroudh.** There are many patisseries in the medina which sell these famous, bite-sized pieces of honey-soaked pastry filled with date paste; try them when you can.

Sbeitla (Sufetula)

Tunisia offers few sights more evocative of past glory than the temples of Roman Sufetula, rising majestically above a rubble-strewn plain, their ancient stone glowing gold in the morning sunshine. This fascinating site lies near the modern town of Sbeitla, 120 km (75 miles) southeast of Kairouan. Little is known about its history; it was probably built by the Romans roughly at the time of Christ, and was later taken by the Byzantines, who built several churches here.

Pomegranates a'plenty—the stalls in Tunisian markets are full of vibrant colour.

The most obvious remains are the three **Capitoline temples,** which tower above the forum. According to traditional Roman practice, the central temple would be dedicated to Jupiter, and those on either side to Juno and Minerva. All three retain the niche in the back wall where the statues of the gods once stood.

The other main attraction at Sbeitla is the Byzantine **Basilica of Vitalis,** which contains a beautiful baptismal font decorated with mosaics and inscribed in Latin.

El Djem

El Djem lies halfway between Sousse and Sfax, surrounded by a plain planted with millions of olive trees. Back in the second century A.D. this was the site of the Roman city of Thysdrus, which grew wealthy on the bounty provided by these trees, selling their harvest of oil to the merchants of Rome.

 Approaching El Djem by road, there can be little doubt as to the town's main attraction, for the **Roman amphitheatre** (built during the third century A.D.) rises majestically above the low houses of the modern city. From whichever direction you approach, it is an extremely impressive sight. As one of the largest amphitheatres in the Roman world—it could seat 30,000—this great coliseum has witnessed many a gory spectacle. After the decline of Thysdrus, it was used throughout the centuries as a fortress by assorted brigands. In 1695, the Turkish bey bombarded the walls in an attempt to oust anti-government rebels holed up within. His work,

We Who Are About to Die

Gladiatorial contests were very popular throughout the Roman Empire, as witnessed by the immense size of amphitheatres such as the one at El Djem. Gladiators were usually slaves or criminals, but those who won often became professionals; the most famous was Spartacus, who led an uprising in 73–71 B.C. On the day of the contest, the gladiators paraded through the amphitheatre, and gave their famous salute to the presiding magistrate: "Ave! Morituri te salutant!" ("Hail! We who are about to die salute you!"). There were many kinds of combatants: the *retarii*, armed with net and trident; the *Thraces*, with small round shield and curved dagger; the *essedarii*, who fought from a chariot; and many more. At the end of a bout, when one of the gladiators was badly wounded, he would raise his forefinger to appeal to the clemency of the crowd—if they waved their handkerchiefs, he would live; but if they pointed their thumbs down (as if plunging a sword into an opponent), crying "Iugula! Iugula!" ("Slay him!"), his end had come.

The imposing amphitheatre of El Djem rises above the surrounding olive orchards.

destructive as it was, benefits the visitor today, by exposing the intricate details of the building's construction — stairways, arches, vaults, buttresses, and underground chambers.

Thysdrus was a lively and prosperous town, almost four times as large as present-day El Djem. At the edge of town on the road to Sfax, evidence of its wealth can still be seen in the striking mosaics on display in the small **museum.** Seashells and birds, peacocks, lions, and tigers are all beautifully portrayed in scenes filled with bright colours. A large mosaic of the young Dionysus, dressed in a leopard skin and mounted on a tigress, is especially impressive.

Situated roughly 65 km (40 miles) south of El Djem is **Sfax,** Tunisia's second largest city (after Tunis) and an important industrial and commercial centre. There is a lively medina here, with fortress-like walls, and an interesting archaeological museum. A ferry to the charming and peaceful **Kerkennah Islands** departs from Sfax port.

☛ DJERBA

As you drive off the little car ferry from Jorf, or cross the causeway from El Kantara, you will be struck by the extreme flatness of Djerba. Most of the island presents a dry, sandy landscape, covered with ancient olive trees, fruit trees, date palms, and grasses. The villages are made up of clusters of little sugar-cube houses, each topped by a hemispherical dome, while the irrigated fields are dotted with straw-hatted men and women, and camels pulling the plough.

Djerba owes its peculiarities to its location. Located deep in the southern part of Tunisia, not far from the border of Libya, the island rests like a huge sandbank in the warm, shallow waters off the coast. There is less than 200 millimeters (8 inches) of rainfall a year; the earth is parched, the dates grown here are of poor quality, fit only for camel fodder, and the crops survive thanks only to irrigation via the hundreds of wells and cisterns that pock the landscape. Nonetheless, the hot, dry weather and white sandy beaches make Djerba a paradise for the sun-worshipping tourists who flock year-round to the hotels of the north coast.

Djerba, along with Majorca and Menorca, claims to be the island of the Lotus Eaters described in Homer's *Odyssey*, where Ulysses' men ate the "fruit of forgetfulness." Legend apart, the first settlers on Djerba were probably Jewish exiles fleeing the destruction of Jerusalem in the sixth century B.C.; their descendants survive in the villages of Hara Kebira and Hara Seghira. The Phoenicians and Romans colonized the island, and built a causeway to link it to the mainland (just to the east of the modern causeway). It was taken by the Arabs in 655, and fought over by the Sicilians, Normans, and Hafsids throughout the Middle Ages. In the 16th century it was used as a base for the notorious Barbary pirates Barbarossa

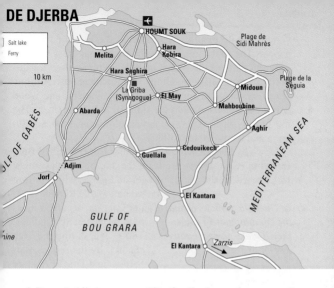

and Dragut Ali (see page 18), finally becoming part of Tunisia during the Ottoman period (see page 19).

Houmt Souk

Houmt Souk is the "capital" of the island, with airline offices, banks, car rental firms, hotels, restaurants, shops, and travel agencies, but even so it is little more than a large village. The town is centred on the **souks,** a maze of tiny alleys and white-washed squares, where stalls are piled high with locally produced crafts—pottery, blankets, coral, and jewellery.

At the edge of town, on the road to the hotel zone, you'll find the **Museum of Popular Arts and Traditions** (*Musée des Arts et Traditions Populaires*). This 18th-century *zaouïa* of Sidi Zitouni, set in a pretty garden, has been converted to hold exhibits which detail the lives of Djerba's people. The first room shows the traditional dress worn in different parts of the island, and the costumes used for important events like weddings or circumcisions. Antique jewellery, manuscript Korans, pottery, joinery, and wood carving are testaments to the skills of local craftsmen. The museum is open daily, except Friday, from 9:00 A.M. to noon and then 3:00 to 6:30 P.M.

Down by the sea is the 15th-century fortress, called **Borj el Kebir** (Great Fort). Built on the site of a 13th-century fort erected by the Sicilian Roger de Lauria (which in turn sat on top of a Roman structure), it was occupied in its time by Spaniards, Hafsids, Turks, and, during the 16th century, by the pirates Barbarossa and Dragut Ali (see page 18).

In Guellala, famous capital of the Djerban pottery trade, they'll make any vase you ask for to order.

In a notorious massacre in 1560, the fort was stormed by Dragut and his men, who ruthlessly put to the sword every single one of the defending Spaniards. In memory of his victory, Dragut built a tower with the skulls and bones of the dead, a grisly monument which survived until 1848, in which year the ex-patriate community persuaded the bey to have it removed. A concrete obelisk in the middle of the parking lot beside the fort marks the site where it stood.

Other Island Sights

To the east of Houmt Souk, the island's best beaches — **Sidi Maharès, Sidi Garous,** and **La Séguia** — stretch for roughly 20 km (12 miles), interrupted only by the rocks of Ras Taguerness. This rocky headland, marked by a tall lighthouse, is the best place on the island for snorkelling and spearfishing.

About 8 km (5 miles) south of Houmt Souk is the island's oldest place of worship, the synagogue of **El Ghriba** (head for the village of Er Riadh, and follow the signs to El Ghriba). The present synagogue was built in the 1920s, and according to local myth it occupies the spot where a holy stone fell to earth in 600 B.C.; it is a place of pilgrimage for Jews from all over North Africa. A wizened sage with a twinkle in his eye will show you the inner sanctum, the oldest part of the synagogue (the foundations may date from the fifth century B.C.), and allow you a glimpse of one of the world's oldest Torahs. You will have to take off your shoes and cover your head before going in. (The synagogue is closed to visitors during Saturday morning services.)

Guellala, on the southern side of the island, is the centre of Djerba's pottery trade. Lining the village's bumpy, unpaved streets are many small potters' workshops, kilns, and factories, each with a small sign inviting tourists to come in and look around. Pots of all descriptions can be bought or made to order, but the artisans of Guellala don't stop there. All sorts of utensils and ornaments are crafted from the pliant clay, and only the master's imagination limits the assortment. Pottery forms Guellala's livelihood, and even broken or spoiled pots don't go to waste. Fences, backyard ovens, kilns, and small sheds and cabins are all put together from chipped or broken pots.

Midoun, Djerba's second biggest community, is basically a market town, hosting a lively open-air souk every Friday. The other weekly attraction is the traditional Berber "wedding" held daily in summer for the benefit of tourists.

SOUTHERN TUNISIA AND THE DESERT

Tunisia is cut in half by a natural depression that runs inland from Gabès to beyond the Algerian border. This trough, which was once an arm of the Mediterranean Sea, cradles a string of huge salt lakes called *chott*, forming a natural barrier to north–south travel. It also marks the boundary between the semiarid steppes of central Tunisia and the true desert of the south.

The largest of these salt lakes, the Chott el Djérid, is also the largest in the whole of the Sahara, covering a staggering area of 5,200 square km (2,000 square miles). Lying to the west and south of the *chott* is the Grand Erg Oriental, a vast ocean of shifting sand dunes, untamed and uninhabited, with the exception of only a few isolated oases.

The oasis towns of Tozeur, Nefta, Kébili, and Douz can all be reached by good roads, either on an organized excursion or by rented car. Tozeur has its own airport, with direct flights from Tunis, Djerba, and Paris.

Gafsa

Travellers who are heading for the Chott el Djérid from Tunis, Sousse, or Kairouan must first pass through the mining town of **Gafsa,** situated at a gap in the mountains, where all the roads south (except the coastal highway) converge. Set in the middle of Tunisia's phosphate-mining region, Gafsa is basically a working city of small businessmen, bureaucrats, and mine workers, built on the site of the Roman town of Capsa. There's not much to see here apart from the **Roman Pools** (*piscines romaines*), a pair of large stone baths filled with sparkling green water. These pools are fed by a hot spring which bubbles up between the ancient stone slabs, and then overflows into the neighbouring *hammam*, and Turkish baths are known.

Near the mining town of **Metlaoui,** on the road from Gafsa to Tozeur, is the spectacular **Seldja Gorge.** A railway runs through the gorge to the town of Redeyef, and in the summer months (July to September) a tourist train called the **Lézard Rouge** (Red Lizard) takes visitors on scenic trips through the ravine. The train was a gift to the bey of Tunis from the French, and its 19th-century carriages have been lovingly restored.

If you have time for a side trip, the remote oases of **Chebika, Tamerza,** and **Midès** are some of the most scenic areas in Tunisia, with deep rock ravines and natural springs cascading from the rock faces. Only Tamerza is accessible by public transport from Redeyef. If you want to go any farther, a four-wheel-drive vehicle is recommended.

The oasis of Tamerza is full of scenic beauty, including deep ravines and water cascading from rocky cliffs.

The town of Gafsa was built in 1434 on the ancient foundations of a Byzantine city called Capsa.

☞ Tozeur and Nefta

The oasis town of **Tozeur** on the northern shore of the Chott el Djérid marks the limit of Roman colonization in Africa. Its name is derived from the Roman settlement of Thusuros, and many a Roman legion stopped at its cool springs on their way from Gabès to Nefta. The town is now the commercial centre of the Djérid region, and is growing quickly —there's even an Arabian Nights theme park. Cars and lorries (trucks) rattle along its sandy streets, while television antennae poke up from the ochre-coloured houses. Beyond this façade of modern prosperity, though, Tozeur still pursues its ancient traditions.

The houses in the **medina** show the local talent for decorative bricklaying, with geometric designs drawn in the traditional flat bricks of sand and clay. Souvenir shops display colourful carpets and rugs bearing stylized human and animal figures. Such patterns are unique to the region and quite unusual for a Muslim town, as Islam forbids the portrayal of men or beasts in any form. Veiled women scuff down the sandy streets to the bustling produce market (by the post office), while villagers who live out of town bargain with shopkeepers for the famous **deglat en-nour** ("fingers of light"). These delicious, plump, sweet dates are grown in the neighbouring palmery and then sold on the branch, or neatly packed in little wooden boxes by the kilo.

During the afternoon heat, you can escape to the cooler surroundings of Tozeur's extensive **palmery,** watered by streams which spring hot from the earth at Ras el Aïoun and ripple through a labyrinth of channels amid a forest of over 200,000 palm trees. The irrigation system was devised by the mathematician Ibn Chabbat in the 13th century, to guarantee that the local landowners all received their equal share of water. Here you can stroll among the shady gardens, or take a guided tour in one of the *calèches* (horse-drawn carriages) that tout for business around the entrance to the palmery.

The road from Tozeur to **Nefta** follows the crest of a low ridge, with the vast Chott el Djérid shimmering in the south. The intense heat and brilliant light create the illusion that the lake is full of water, but it's just a mirage: the lake only has water in it after very heavy rains—a rare occurrence in this arid region.

From the high ground which holds Nefta's buildings, you can look down into a bowl-shaped depression carpeted in palm trees and watered by innumerable springs. This is the famous **Corbeille** (Basket) of Nefta, a lush and fragrant garden where the hot desert wind becomes a cool and soothing breeze, and the sound of trickling water relaxes the weary traveller. It's a surprise to see such fertile abundance in the middle of so desolate a landscape—dates, figs, bananas, peppers, and pomegranates are all flourishing underneath a lush green canopy of palms.

Due to the many *koubbas* (saints' tombs) and mosques in the area, Nefta has been something of a place of pilgrimage for some years, earning it the title of "Kairouan of the Desert." Be warned that on religious holidays the town is particularly busy, and accommodation may be hard to find.

Take your fill of dates in Douz, at one of the many roadside markets.

Kébili and Douz

A good road leads southeast from Tozeur, and follows a causeway traversing the endless salt flats of the **Chott el Djérid**. The causeway runs dead straight for nearly 40 km (25 miles) across a blinding, blue-white expanse of crusted salt, stained here and there with pink and green: the monotony relieved only by a few intrepid souvenir sellers at the roadside. The hot air creates strange optical illusions, and oncoming traffic gradually materializes out of a shimmering haze. As you approach the southern shore, drifts of blowing sand begin to encroach on the tarmac, and you realise that you have arrived at the edge of the Sahara Desert.

The first town you come to, 96 km (60 miles) from Tozeur, is the dusty military camp of **Kébili.** Two picturesque old desert strongholds have been converted to hotel-restaurants, where you can dine among the ghosts of the Foreign Legion. Until just over a century ago, Kébili was a notorious market for slaves brought from south of the Sahara.

Farther on from Kébili, barriers made of palm fronds fight a losing battle to prevent the fringing dunes of the Grand Erg Oriental drifting across the highway. An avenue of fragrant eucalyptus trees marks the approach to **Douz,** the self-styled "Gateway to the Sahara" and a major centre for camel trips and Land Rover excursions into the desert. The town is at its busiest on Thursday, when the semi nomadic tribesmen from surrounding oases come to trade at the market. The market square is crammed with men in brown burnouses and white head cloths, most of them haggling over sacks of wool, bundles of camel fodder, piles of beans, and bunches of dates. Cafés are crowded, the tiny local bakery turns out dozens upon dozens of delicious fresh loaves, and everyone joins in the spirit of the usual weekly festivities.

Camel-back excursions into the Sahara leave from the "gateway" of Douz.

Just a few minutes walk from the market square, you will find the **camel market,** where buyers and sellers haggle animatedly over the long-suffering beasts. "How is it possible," the buyer will ask, "that this poor decrepit thing can be offered for sale?

I would not give the husk of a fig for it!" The seller, who is, quite naturally, incensed by such effrontery, insists that the beast is barely out of the womb, certainly not yet in its prime. "Disease is a thing foreign to it, as God is my witness!" Then the camel may voice its opinion with a raucous bellow, giving a definite sign of life quickly picked up on by both antagonists as a bargaining-point.

The Oasis — A Desert Paradise

To the people of the desert, an oasis — a "plot of paradise in the midst of an inferno" — is more than just a watering place. It takes ingenuity and painstaking, meticulous labour to make the desert bloom. Each rivulet of precious water is coaxed and diverted into the bottom land. The soil is tilled and fertilized, and eventually a palmery (palm grove), essential for shade, is created. Soon the oasis-dweller's meagre diet of dates and camel's milk is augmented with grain, figs, apricots, and a few root vegetables grown among the palms. All refuse, including camel dung, is ploughed back into the soil, and every square metre of shaded earth is used for cultivation. The village houses are built on higher land, exposed to the merciless sun. Finally, the palmery matures into a garden paradise with a full range of fruit, vegetables, animal fodder, and flowers.

The palm tree is the heart and soul of the oasis, and every part of it is used. The trunks provide bridges across the irrigation channels, and are used as roof beams in houses; the fibres that grow around its base make stuffing for saddles; the fronds are woven into mats and baskets; the heavy base of the leaf stalk is used as a beater by the washerwomen; and the sap is fermented to make the palm wine called *laghmi*.

*The ancient stronghold of Kébili at the Saharan border:
once a slave market, this is now a peaceful site to visit.*

In the last days of December, Douz comes alive with the
Festival of the Sahara, seven days of camel fights, shooting
contests, greyhound races, and traditional music and dance.
Poets test their powers of improvisation in a *joute poétique*
(poetry "jousting match"), and horsemen from the surrounding regions gather to stage a *fantasia*, a mock battle-charge
in which mounted tribesmen thunder down on the audience,
spurred on by rifle shots and war cries, only to turn and retreat at the last moment.

Gabès

The road east from Kébili to Gabès crosses a dry and dusty
plain which separates the salt lake of Chott el Fedjedj and
the jagged summits of the Djébel Tebaga mountains. At **El
Hamma** there are hot sulphur baths which were once used
by the Romans.

The different tribes of the Gabès oasis come together at the central square in Douz, for the weekly market.

Gabès is a large industrial town, known as the "Gateway to the South" because all highway traffic from north to south must pass through it. Although hotels, restaurants, and a resort complex make the new town seem much the same as any other along the Tunisian coast, Gabès actually has the added attraction of a huge palmery right beside the sea.

The Gabès **oasis** is so large that a dozen separate villages lie hidden in its shady depths, with a serpentine road winding through the palms and linking them together. The classic way to tour this forest of 300,000 palms is by *calèche* (horse-drawn carriage); you can hire one at the tourist office in the centre of town. The coastal climate is too cool and moist to produce top quality dates; the Gabès palm trees are grown primarily for shade, allowing crops and fruit trees to be cultivated in the oasis gardens. The palm trunks are used for construction, while the dates provide animal fodder. Most *calèche* tours head up to the village of Chenini, where you can shop for handicrafts.

Matmata

In the hills 40 km (25 miles) to the south of Gabès lies **Matmata,** one of the most unusual villages in Tunisia. If you have seen the films *The English Patient* or *Star Wars*, then you have seen Matmata—the cave scenes and the archaeological digs in *English Patient* and the scene in which Luke Skywalker goes back to the underground house where he grew up were filmed here. Matmata is a troglodyte village, where the locals have created subterranean homes by excavating chambers in the soft earth.

Most of their **cave houses** follow a basic design—a circular pit about 10 metres (33 feet) across, with a sloping tunnel leading from the floor to ground level. This sunken "courtyard" has a number of rooms leading off, used variously as bedchambers, animal pens, and storerooms. The larger houses may have two or three courtyards linked by tunnels. These unusual dwellings are very practical: the insulation provided by the earth keeps the rooms cool in summer and warm in winter. The tradition of living underground goes back a long way—the Greek historian Herodotus records the existence of troglodytes in this region in the fourth century B.C.

The people of Matmata are Berbers, and they work hard to glean a livelihood from the dry soil. Olive trees, figs, barley, and a few stunted palms grow in the shady ravines that cleave the hillsides. The discovery of Matmata by the outside

Shelter from the beating sun: visit the curious troglodyte homes of Matmata.

world has added a new element to the tenuous local economy—souvenir shops, restaurants, and camel rides have taken over as the primary source of income. Most villagers now live above ground and levy a fee for looking inside their former homes.

Three **hotels** have been set up in disused cave dwellings. The rooms are small and primitive, with few amenities other than rickety beds and a bare light bulb, but a night spent in one of these underground hotels is an experience simply not to be missed.

From the Hotel Les Berbères a new tarmac road leads west to the villages of Tamezret, Taoujou, and Zeraoua. Tamezret, 10 km (6 miles) away, is a compact village of above-ground stone houses clustered around the mosque. You can enjoy the view from the hilltop café while sipping almond tea.

Medenine and the Ksar Villages

The mountains which stretch south from Matmata were one of Tunisia's last strongholds of Berber culture. When hostile Arab tribes swept across North Africa during the 11th century, sacking villages and destroying farms to make pasture for their camels, the indigenous Berbers took to the hills, and sought refuge in fortified villages. In time many returned to the plains and were assimilated into Tunisian Arab culture, but a few remained in their mountain strongholds, keeping alive the language and traditions of their ancestors. By the 19th century, however, spoken Berber had survived only in a handful of villages, and Berber culture had as good as disappeared. Today, the unique architecture of the fortified *ksar* villages in the hills to the west of Medenine stands as a monument to a past way of life.

Roughly 75 km (47 miles) south of Gabès, the town of **Medenine** was once a major grain depot, and its complex of

Kalaâ, Ghorfas, and Ksour

When the Berbers first fled to the mountains they built crude hilltop forts, called *kalaâ*, on the crags above their villages, as protection from the marauding Arabs. The *kalaâ* of Douiret is particularly impressive, perched on top of a 700-metre- (2,296-foot-) high peak.

A *ghorfa* is a Berber granary—a long rectangular room topped by a barrel-vaulted roof. The vault was made by piling earth-filled sacks into the right shape, bending olive branches over the top, and adding a roof of stone, mortar, and clay; the sacks were removed when the roof had set. Very often *ghorfas* were constructed in rows, one on top of another, and honeycomb-like complexes of three, four, or more storeys were not unusual. For protection, *ghorfas* were built around a rectangular courtyard to form a fortified communal granary called a *ksar* (plural *ksour*). In times of peace, the villagers would gather at the *ksar* to pray and socialize, as well as trade at the weekly market. When danger threatened, they would all take refuge within the protection of its fortress-like outer walls.

35 *ksour*, up to six storeys in height, held in the region of 8,000 *ghorfas* (fortified stone houses that once held the grain). Today there are only a few dozen *ghorfas* remaining, grouped around three courtyards, one of which has been converted into a shopping centre for tourists. On the outskirts of town in the village of **Metameur,** a picturesque *ksar* has been converted into a recommended hotel (see page 131).

To visit the *ksar* villages without a four-wheel-drive vehicle, you will have to drive south to Tataouine first, where a number of tarmac roads head into the

The mosque of Métameur, near Médenine, overlooks an old ksar.

hills. **Chenini** is the nearest and most popular with tour buses, an attractive village set high up in a rocky valley. A tiny white mosque sits on the pass above the village, but the rest of the buildings seem almost to blend into the rock. Constructed from the local stone, and built along the natural rock strata, they were well camouflaged against marauding Arabs as they approached from the valleys below. The "back rooms" are hollowed out of the soft rock, and shielded from view by a row of *ghorfas* facing inwards. Chenini is still inhabited, but many of the villagers now live in the newer houses lower down the valley.

Close by, **Douiret** can be reached by an unsurfaced road from Chenini, or on a tarmac road which leaves the highway about 8 km south of Tataouine. The village makes an impressive sight, with a ruined *kalaâ* (fortress) perched atop a 700-metre- (2,296-foot-) high peak, and two terraces of houses spread out below around the white-washed mosque. Many of the *ghorfas* have been kept in good repair, and you can also see an underground oil press near the mosque.

If you go back to the road to Chenini, a right fork leads to **Ghoumrassen,** a market town which holds a lively souk on Friday. The town is famous in Tunisia for its doughnuts— *ftair*—which can be bought in one of the many patisseries on the main street (*ftair* can also be found in towns all over the country, in shops belonging to Ghoumrassen emigrants). The town is set in a steep-sided valley, and rows of cave houses have been carved into the cliffs and spurs of the upper slopes.

The remarkable ghorfas of Ksar Haddada used to hold stores of grain.

From here, a road branches left to the smaller village of **Guermessa,** where a narrow, rocky footpath climbs to the *kalaâ*, perched above town. In **Ksar Haddada,** 6 km (4 miles) north of Ghoumrassen, the village *ksar* has been converted into a comfortable hotel.

WHAT TO DO

SHOPPING

The souks of Tunisia are less exotic than those of Morocco, and have largely been taken over by souvenir shops. The best places to track down authentic crafts are the souks of Tunis, Sousse, Kairouan, and Houmt Souk. Country towns have a weekly general market, a lively and colourful spectacle worth visiting whether you intend buying anything or not.

Shops are generally open daily from 8:00 A.M. to 12:30 P.M. and 2:30 to 6:00 P.M., although they may close for short periods on Friday, the Muslim holy day. The souks are at their liveliest in the early morning and late afternoon.

Bargaining

In a place where many products are handmade, each item has a different value depending on the quality of workmanship. Bargaining is thus a way of determining an appropriate price, not simply a way for the shopkeeper to get more money from the buyer. To ensure the best price, you should get to know the market by browsing in several shops.

When you find something you want to buy, ask the shopkeeper how much it costs, and then offer around half of what you're prepared to pay. Keep haggling until you settle on a mutually acceptable price. If the item is expensive—a carpet or a leather jacket, for instance—the process might involve several glasses of mint tea and a good half hour of your time. Two golden rules are never to begin bargaining for something you do not genuinely intend to buy, and never mention a price that you are not prepared to pay.

In the resorts on the coast, many traders are aware that some tourists feel uncomfortable with bargaining, and will quote you their "best price" straight away if you ask them to. This is the minimum they are prepared to accept, and you will probably be wasting your time if you try to force them any lower. Competition between shops is traditionally fierce, and many traders are forced to work on very narrow profit margins.

If you prefer not to bargain, you can visit the local O.N.A.T. (*Organisation Nationale de L'Artisanat Tunisien*) shop, a state-run crafts shop which has fixed prices (ask at the tourist office for the address of the nearest ones). At these shops you gain an idea of

These ancient vessels, called amphora, are still frequently used to carry water.

the range of crafts offered, and the prices you can expect to pay; but remember that in the souks the variety will be greater, and the prices slightly lower. Many shops will ship your purchases home if they are too bulky for you to take on the plane; however, it is recommended that you plan to bring back your purchases personally, in order to avoid long shipping delays or complications.

What to Buy

Pottery and ceramics. Tunisia's main pottery-producing areas are Nabeul and Djerba, but their wares are available all around the country. Nabeul is famed for its Andalusian-style

The colourful Tunisian souks set out a large selection of handicrafts to lure the prospective buyer.

ceramics, such as bowls, vases, and decorative panels, with intricate designs in blue, yellow, and green on a white background. Djerba produces terra-cotta ware, ranging from small bowls to huge amphorae. It also produces traditional green and yellow kitchenware; the colours are said to represent a palm tree: green for the leaves and yellow for the dates.

Carpets. Tunisian carpets are not as high in quality as their more famous counterparts from Turkey and Iran; they will never be family heirlooms, but they are attractive and competitively priced. Carpet making is controlled by the O.N.A.T., and all carpets have to be stamped on the back with one of three grades—*Deuxième Choix* (second choice), *Premier Choix* (first choice), or *Qualité Supérieure* (superior quality), according to the number of knots per square metre. There are two basic patterns: bright, multicoloured designs in blue and red; and geometric designs in wool colours such as cream, beige, brown, and black. The best shops for buying carpets are in Kairouan and Tunis, where shopkeepers will invite you to watch their carpet-makers at work. Seeing the skill and labour involved will help you to understand the prices asked for them.

Mergoums are carpets that are made by weaving as opposed to knotting, with colourful geometric patterns on a solid background (usually yellow-brown); they are traditionally woven by the southern Tunisian Berbers, in the bright reds and purples of the shawls worn by Berber women. Mergoums are sold mainly in the south, in Gafsa, Tozeur, Gabès, and Djerba.

Jewellery. Tunisia's jewellery was traditionally produced by the country's Jewish community; the best places to buy gold and silver are still in the old Jewish areas of Djerba and Tunis. Popular designs include a fish motif and the Hand of Fatimah, both of which are believed to ward off evil spirits. More difficult to find is traditional Berber silver—chunky bracelets, earrings, and brooches, inset with semi-precious stones; try the shops in El Djem or Tozeur. In Tabarka you will find coral jewellery, but remember that coral is an endangered species: you might think twice before buying it.

You will find an exceptional selection of jewellery in Djerba and Tunis.

Leather goods. These include *babouches* (Tunisian slippers), handbags, belts, purses, wallets, skirts, trousers, and jackets. Price and quality both vary widely —a lot of the goods on offer

in the popular tourist resorts can be shoddy, so check the standard of craftsmanship carefully before you buy. For better quality leather products, try the shops in Tunis.

Woodwork and metalwork. The olive-growing region of the Sahel produces attractive items made from carved olive wood—bowls, chess sets, jewellery boxes, and backgammon boards. Tunisian brassware is often low quality, but personalized teapots, plates, coffeepots, and trays make attractive souvenirs. Rather more original are the ornate filigree bird cages from Sidi Bou Saïd.

SPORTS AND OTHER ACTIVITIES

Watersports

With more than 1,000 km (620 miles) of coastline, and some of the finest beaches in the Mediterranean, Tunisia is truly a paradise for watersports enthusiasts. The perfect white sands, and the warm, shallow waters of Hammamet, Nabeul, Sousse, Monastir, and Djerba are just right for safe, sheltered **swimming,** ideal for children. In addition, most of the resort hotels have their own heated swimming pools.

The shallow, sheltered waters also mean that Tunisia's beaches are the ideal place to learn **windsurfing**—there are boards for hire and instructors on all the main beaches. Other activities offered to enthusiasts on the beach include **parasailing, dinghy sailing,** and **water-skiing.**

Tunisia's rocky north coast is good **snorkelling** territory, and if you feel the urge to go deeper, **scuba-diving** instruction is available at Tabarka, Port el Kantaoui, and Monastir. Cap Bon is a favourite area for spearfishing, especially at Kélibia and Sidi Daoud. Scuba divers might want to explore this part of the coast, which is noted for its rich underwater life. For spearfishing, a permit is required, from the *Di-*

Land Rover safaris offer a comfortable opportunity to explore the Sahara.

recteur des Pêches. A travel agent can obtain this for you and explain the formalities.

Sea Angling

If you fish, feel free to cast a line from the rocks anywhere you like; a licence is not necessary for fishing in Tunisia. For deep-water angling, boats can be hired from the marinas at Port el Kantaoui and Monastir. Among the fish found inshore are mullet, bream, and sea bass, while offshore anglers can expect tunny, dorado, and shark.

Desert Safaris

Any travel agent will have details of organized Land Rover tours around southern Tunisia, ranging from two-day excursions to Matmata and the *ksar* villages to ten-day "safaris" deep into the desert. Tours can be booked on the spot in Hammamet, Sousse, Gabès, Djerba, and Douz, but longer trips should be arranged in advance. Some adventure holiday companies in the U.K. offer all-inclusive safaris. Contact the O.N.T.T. (*office National du Tourisme Tunisien*) (see page 123) for details.

Sand Yachting

You can try out this exciting sport on the salt flats of the Chott el Djérid. The "yacht" is a three-wheeled vehicle fitted with a mast and sail, and it can attain a speed of over 50 km/h (30 mph) in the strong desert winds. Contact the Hotel El Djérid in Tozeur for details.

Horseback Riding and Camel Treks

Fine Arab horses and ponies can be hired for a canter along the beaches at Sousse, Djerba, and Hammamet, at reasonable prices. More serious riding can be arranged through your hotel or the local tourist office.

Beautiful courses and guaranteed sun—the Tunisian climate is ideal for golf and other outdoor activities.

You can try the delights of camel riding along the majority of tourist beaches, and at the oasis communities of Tozeur and Douz. The latter also offer guided, multi-day camel treks into the desert, travelling from well to well and camping in nomad tents. For full details contact the O.N.T.T. (see page 123).

Hunting

Tunisia is famous for its wild boar, which can be hunted in season (November to January) in the hills of Cap Bon, and in the forests around Tabarka and Aïn Draham. Licences and import permits for firearms must be organised through a travel agent well in advance. Further details are available from the O.N.T.T. (see page 123).

Tennis and Golf

The first golf course in Tunisia was built at La Soukra, near Tunis, in 1924, and is still welcoming visitors. There are five other courses: the championship level at Port el Kantaoui, which hosts the Tunisian Open every April; a brand new course at Tabarka; another at two challenging courses at Hammamet and Monastir. Equipment and caddies can be hired, and advance reservations are recommended. Some package tour companies also offer golfing holidays in Tunisia; for details contact a travel agent or the O.N.T.T. (see page 123).

Bird-Watching

During spring and autumn millions of migratory birds pass through Tunisia on their way to and from their summer nesting grounds in Europe, making use of the short sea crossing between Cap Bon and Sicily. The most impressive species are the birds of prey, which include sparrow hawks, peregrine falcons, buzzards, eagles, and kites. For closer inspection, the peregrines nest on the crags at the cape, and there is a falconry centre at nearby El Haouaria (see page 50).

Good places to see wading birds, especially flamingo, avocet, and spoonbill, are the lagoons (known as *sebkhet*) and salt-marshes that fringe the eastern coast.

Lac Ichkeul National Park, near Bizerte, is North Africa's most important waterfowl site, providing a wintering ground for many varieties of waders, duck, and geese. The best time to visit is between October and February. Rare birds on the lake include the white-headed duck and purple gallinule.

ENTERTAINMENT

You will always be able to find plenty to do in Tunisia, and for added entertainment most of the resort hotels put on shows for their guests.

Nightlife

Most resort hotels have their own bars, nightclubs, and discotheques, and many will also arrange tours to small nightspots in nearby towns. In addition they may arrange a *soirée folklorique* (folklore evening) each week, at which a typical Tunisian dinner is accompanied by local folk music, snake charmers, dancing, and maybe a belly dancer as well.

Outside the resorts, Tunis is the only place that offers European-style bars or clubs, most of them in the streets around avenue Bourguiba. There is also a lively café society in the coastal suburbs of Sidi Bou Saïd and La Marsa. Nightlife in the smaller towns consists of a stroll along the main avenue, followed by an animated conversation in one of the various sidewalk cafés.

Nightlife everywhere perks up during Ramadan (see page 90), when all Muslims do not eat or drink during daylight hours. For four weeks, the evening is a time for feasting and celebrations which last well into the small hours. You don't have to abstain during the day to join in at night.

Hammamet has an International Cultural Centre, where dramatic and musical events are held in the opulent grounds of a luxurious former private estate. Displays of traditional Tunisian music and dance are regularly staged in the romantic setting of Hammamet's medieval kasbah, and at the *ribats* of Sousse and Monastir.

Folklore

One of the shows which is regularly staged for tourists is a traditional wedding—a Tunisian bride dressed for her wedding is a splendid sight. Her costume is made of variegated silks and cloth of gold and silver, all set off by a veritable king's ransom in jewellery—rings, bangles, earrings, head-dresses, necklaces, brooches, belts, and sashes—and her hands and feet are decorated with henna patterned in intricate, lacy designs.

Real weddings are traditionally held in the summer, when relatives who have gone to work abroad come home

---

Calendar of Events

Exact dates should be confirmed through local tourist offices.

June. *El Haouaria, Cap Bon:* Falconry Festival—staged displays of falconry.

Dougga: Dougga Festival—drama at the Roman theatre.

July–August. *Carthage, near Tunis:* Carthage International Festival—music, dance, and drama.

Tabarka: Tabarka Festival—music, crafts display.

Houmt Souk, Djerba: Festival of Ulysses—music and dancing.

August. *Hammamet:* Hammamet Festival—concerts and plays staged at the International Cultural Centre.

Sousse: Festival of Baba Aoussou—carnival procession.

November. *Carthage, near Tunis:* Carthage Film Festival—new films from the Third World; held every two years.

Tozeur: Oasis Festival—displays of folklore, oasis agriculture, camel racing, fantasias.

December. *Douz:* Festival of the Sahara—folk music, dancing, camel racing, *fantasias.* Late December.

---

for a holiday. Processions of merrymakers in cars and trucks wind through the town on a wedding day, honking on horns, banging on drums, and playing the pipes. Celebrations may last for as long as a week, and visitors are more than welcome to join in the festivities—in Tunisia, weddings are public events at which everyone is encouraged to join in whether they are acquainted with the happy couple or not.

Festivals

Tunisia's major national festivals are all religious in nature. The dates they fall on are determined by the lunar calendar, with the result that each time they fall about 11 days earlier than the previous year (see page 121).

A number of Tunisian hotels offer evenings of music and traditional dance.

For the month of **Ramadan,** all Muslims must abstain from eating, drinking, smoking, and sex during the hours of daylight; exceptions are made for travellers, children, pregnant women, and warriors engaged in a *jihad* (holy war). As soon as the sun sets, however, that all changes, and the evenings are given over to eating, drinking, and revelry— street entertainment is often staged in the form of travelling musicians and puppet shows. The end of Ramadan is marked by the feast of **Aïd es-Seghir** (also called **Aïd el-Fitr**), which is a national holiday.

Aïd el-Kebir (or **Aïd el-Idha**) is a commemoration of Abraham's test of faith, when God commanded him to sacrifice his son Isaac. It is a time for family reunions, at which many families will slaughter a sheep in tribute to Abraham's trial. The feast of **Mouloud,** which marks the birthday of the Prophet Mohammed, is accompanied by special prayers and ceremonies. In particular it is a major festival for the holy city of Kairouan.

There are many other festivals during the year, including harvest festivals and arts festivals (see page 89).

CHILDREN

Tunisia makes a good destination for a family holiday. The sandy beaches and sheltered shallow waters along the east coast offer a safe playground for children of all ages, while the resorts offer all kinds of facilities to entertain the younger ones, including beach games, paddling pools, camel rides, video games, table tennis, volleyball courts, miniature golf, sand-castle contests, discotheques for children under 16, and sometimes a snake-charmer show once a week. The better hotels also have a child-minding service so that parents can have an evening to themselves.

Thanks to the soft sand on its fine beaches, Tunisia is a child's paradise.

EATING OUT

The dishes that make up a traditional Tunisian dinner reflect the culinary influences of the different peoples who have occupied the country in centuries past—couscous from the original Berbers, olives and olive oil from the Romans, coffee and spices from the Arabs, and honey-soaked pastries from the Turks. The French introduced restaurants and the idea of separate courses (eating out was not part of traditional Tunisian culture). In fact, the best way that you can sample true Tunisian cuisine is as a guest in a Tunisian home; but only a lucky few will receive such an invitation.

The terrace of a sidewalk café is the best place to enjoy the street atmosphere.

Where to Eat

You can choose from a range of eating places. First there is the basic café-restaurant called a *gargotte*, aimed primarily at local people, perhaps with a few tables set out on the pavement. It serves cheap, solid fare such as couscous, meatballs, soup, salad, and bread, at very low prices. Even cheaper is the *rôtisserie*, a Tunisian-style fast-food stall, where you can fill up for about a dinar; they serve mostly fried food, which you eat standing up at the counter. In the tourist resorts, European-style fast-food restaurants sell the usual burgers, chips (fries), and pizzas.

Then there are the French-style cafés and *pâtisseries* that you'll find in the larger cities and tourist towns, where you can enjoy a croissant, cake, or pastry washed down with coffee, mint tea, or fruit juice. Top of the range are the European-style restaurants offering a mix of Tunisian, French, and Italian dishes. There is little to choose between most of them in terms of food, but prices vary according to decor and location—the nearer the waterfront, the higher the prices. Perhaps best of all are the seafood restaurants along the coast.

Away from the cities and resorts there are very few restaurants; if you are travelling off the beaten track, you will generally end up eating at your hotel. Women travelling alone should be aware that once you get away from the tourist resorts, cafés become a strictly male preserve—a woman on her own is likely to attract a lot of unwanted attention.

Meal Times

Breakfast. Breakfast in the resort hotels is usually a self-service buffet; in smaller hotels you will be given a pot of coffee, fruit juice, and a basket of croissants, pastries, bread, butter, and jam. Breakfast is generally served between 7:00 and 9:30 A.M. As a change from the hotel, you might like to join the locals in the *pâtisserie*, and enjoy a coffee and croissant, or perhaps a traditional doughnut-like fritter, known as *ftair*, at a sidewalk table.

Lunch and dinner. Lunch is eaten between 12:00 noon and 3:00 P.M., while dinner is served between about 7:00 and 9:00 P.M. In areas away from Tunis and the tourist resorts, you are unlikely to find anywhere still serving food after 9:30 P.M.

The standard Tunisian dinner offered at tourist restaurants consists of *chorba* (soup) followed by *brik* (stuffed pastry), and then a main course of couscous, before finishing off with a dessert of fresh fruit and *maqroudh* (sweetmeats). All Tunisian meals are accompanied by a small dish of oily, red piquant sauce called *harissa*—beware, it is very hot!

Classic Tunisian Dishes

Appetizers. The most common starter is *chorba*, an oily, peppery soup thickened with pasta. Also very popular is *salade méchouia*, which is not a salad at all, but a delicious cold dish of roasted sweet peppers, tomatoes, and onions, all garnished with chunks of tuna and hard-boiled egg. For a uniquely Tunisian dish, try the *brik à l'œuf*, a pastry envelope containing an egg, sealed and fried in olive oil until crisp, and eaten with your fingers. This requires skill! In up-market restaurants, you'll find *brik* served with other fillings, such as vegetables and seafood.

Other starters include *brochettes*, small cubes of lamb grilled on skewers, and *kefta*, meatballs of minced lamb with cumin and coriander, cooked on a charcoal grill. A *salade tunisienne* (Tunisian salad) is usually a finely chopped mixture of cucumber, green pepper, tomato, and onion, dressed with oil and vinegar and then flavoured with fresh coriander. *Merguez* is tasty spicy beef or lamb sausage.

Couscous. It's just about impossible to visit Tunisia without coming across the local staple, couscous. It consists of a heap of steamed semolina grains which are topped with stewed vegetables and meat. Every housewife and chef has his or her own private recipe. The meat is usually chicken or lamb, and the vegetables are carrot, chick peas, squash, and courgette, all flavoured with herbs and spices. If you prefer, it's always possible to ask for your couscous *"sans viande"* (without meat), though vegetarians should be aware that the vegetables have probably been cooked in meat stock.

A traditional Tunisian meal always starts with brik à l'œuf, a tasty envelope of pastry filled with egg.

Kamounia. This is a chicken, lamb, or beef casserole, cooked long and slow, and strongly flavoured with cumin. You will have to visit one of the better restaurants to find it.

Odjja. If you've never tried brains, you might get your chance if *odjja* is on the menu. Small pieces of meat, fish, or brains are cooked in a sauce of tomatoes, hot peppers, garlic, mint, coriander, and caraway, and scrambled with eggs to make a tasty and unusual dish.

Tajine. Tunisian *tajines* are based on a vegetable-and-egg mixture cooked in an earthenware casserole—similar to a quiche, but without the pastry. They are often flavoured with spinach or cheese.

Koucha Fil Kolla. A lamb casserole sprinkled with rosemary and spices, baked in its own juices in a sealed clay pot. The pot is ceremonially broken open at your table.

Doulma. A dish with Turkish origins: green peppers or marrow (squash) are stuffed with meat, parsley, onion, and egg.

Fish and seafood. The fertile waters off Tunisia provide a rich harvest of fish. Red mullet (*rouget*), sea bream

Even though generally sold by the pound, just a few magroudh are enough for a good snack.

(*daurade*), sardines, tuna (*thon*), grouper (*merou*), and sea bass (*loup de mer*) head the list. Fish can be used in *odjja* or couscous, but is more often simply grilled or poached and served alone as a main course.

Tunisian waters also yield a wonderful selection of seafood (*fruits de mer*), particularly octopus (*poulpe*), squid (*calamar*), and prawns (*crevette*). A popular starter is *brik aux fruits de mer*, a *brik* filled with prawns and flaked fish in a sauce of cream and white wine.

Desserts. Fresh fruit—melons, tangerines, peaches, figs, dates, and apricots—is often served to round off a meal, but when it comes to desserts, the Tunisians have a very sweet tooth. A classic sweet is baklava, which is alternating layers of thin pastry and ground almonds soaked with honey. The holy city of Kairouan is famous for *maqroudh*, little cakes of honey-soaked semolina pastry stuffed with date paste. *Assi-*

da is a sweet custard with hazelnuts, milk, and eggs, decorated with pistachios, crushed hazelnuts, and pine nuts, and served as a special treat on festive occasions.

Drinks

Coffee is available in French-style cafés, and is generally served strong and black (*café express*). If you would like an espresso with milk added, ask for *crème express*. For a large, milky coffee, you should order *café au lait*. There's also *café turc* (Turkish style), black and sweet, served with the grounds in a tiny cup.

Mint tea, or *thé vert*, is a delicious and refreshing drink which is made from an infusion of green tea with sprigs of fresh mint, sweetened with sugar. It is usually served in small tulip-shaped glasses. Ordinary tea, *thé rouge*, is stewed for hours, and is served very strong and very sweet.

Although Islam forbids the consumption of alcohol, wine, beer, and spirits are available in hotels, bars, and restaurants in tourist resorts. **Mineral water** (*eau minérale*) is available in all restaurants; still (*non gazeuse*) or sparkling (*gazeuse*).

The Tea-Making Ceremony

In a Tunisian home, the honour of the friendly ritual of the tea-making ceremony usually falls to an important guest.

The curvy teapot of silver, pewter, or enamel is rinsed with boiling water. Green tea and a sprig of mint are jammed into the pot and scalded with a small amount of boiling water, which is swished around and then poured away. Sugar is added, and the pot filled with boiling water from a copper kettle. It infuses for a few minutes, then the teapot is held high, a glass is filled, and the contents poured back into the pot. A second glass is filled and tasted for sweetness, more sugar is added if necessary, and the tea, finally, is served.

Tunisian **wines** are fairly palatable, and well worth trying. The Phoenicians planted vineyards soon after they colonized Tunisia, so the country can claim more than two thousand years of wine-production history. The Romans extended and refined the art, but the coming of Islam forced most vineyards to sell their wares as fruit rather than wine. During the French Protectorate the industry was revived and updated. Among the reds, *Coteaux de Hammamet* and *Magon* are especially good, while *Sidi Rais* is a worthwhile white. Unique among Tunisian wines is *Muscat Sec de Kélibia*, a medium-dry white wine made with the muscat grape usually used for sweet wines.

Many French aperitifs and liqueurs appear in cafés and bars, but are more expensive than local products. *Thibarine* is a Tunisian date liqueur similar to *Cointreau*, while *Boukha* is a dry fig brandy. In Djerba you may be offered the local fire-water, *laghmi,* made with the fermented sap of the palm tree.

The only widely available Tunisian beer is a rather watery light lager called *Celtia*.

To Help You Order ...

Do you have a set-price menu? **Avez-vous un menu à prix fixe?**

I'd like a/an/some… **J'aimerais…**

beer	**une bière**	pepper	**du poivre**
bread	**du pain**	rice	**du riz**
coffee	**un café**	salad	**de la salade**
fish	**du poisson**	salt	**du sel**
fork	**une fourchette**	soup	**de la soupe**
glass	**un verre**	spoon	**une cuiller**
ice cream	**une glace**	sugar	**du sucre**
knife	**un couteau**	tea	**un thé**
meat	**de la viande**	(mint)	**(à la menthe)**
mineral water	**de l'eau**	wine	**du vin**

... and Read the Menu

agneau	lamb	**fraises**	strawberries
ail	garlic	**fromage**	cheese
ananas	pineapple	**(de chèvre)**	(goat's)
artichaut	artichoke	**gâteau**	cake
anchois	anchovies	**homard**	lobster
asperges	asparagus	**huile**	oil
aubergine	eggplant	**huîtres**	oysters
beurre	butter	**légumes**	vegetables
biftek	beefsteak	**merguez**	spicy sausage
bœuf	beef	**moules**	mussels
boulettes	meatballs	**moutarde**	mustard
brochette	skewered meat or fish	**mouton**	mutton
calmar	squid	**noix**	nuts
carottes	carrots	**nouilles**	noodles
champignons	mushrooms	**œufs**	eggs
chorba	soup	**oignons**	onions
chou	cabbage	**pample-mousse**	grapefruit
chou-fleur	cauliflower	**pêche**	peach
citron	lemon	**persil**	parsley
concombre	cucumber	**poire**	pear
confiture	jam	**pois chiches**	chickpeas
côtelettes d'agneau	lamb chops	**pomme**	apple
		poulet	chicken
crevettes	shrimps	**raisins**	grapes
dattes	dates	**rognons**	kidneys
daurade	dorado, sea bream	**saucisse**	sausage
		saumon	salmon
épinards	spinach	**thon**	tuna fish
figues	figs	**tomate**	tomato
foie	liver	**veau**	veal

99

INDEX

HANDY TRAVEL TIPS

A

ACCOMMODATION *(logement; hôtel)* (See also CAMPING, YOUTH HOSTELS, and the list of RECOMMENDED HOTELS)

Resort Hotels. Resort hotels are usually first class, well run, and reasonably priced—especially if your room is included as part of a package tour. Single rooms can be expensive.

Hotels. All major towns have a good range of **hotels,** and it's usually possible to find both bargain and luxury accommodation. All hotels are rated by the National Tourist Office (*Office National du Tourisme Tunisian*, or O.N.T.T.; see page 123), ranging from one to four stars, plus a 4-star-deluxe (****L) category. Rates should be quoted to you with service and taxes included, and prices must by law be posted in each room (usually on the back of the door). Prices are considerably cheaper during the low season, between October and May.

Marhalas. The Touring Club of Tunisia and the Tunisian government have established *marhalas* (simple inns) in historic buildings. In Houmt Souk, Kairouan, and Nefta, they are in converted *caravanserais;* in Matmata one is in a troglodyte dwelling; and in the far south several *ksars* (fortified villages) have been converted.

a single/double room	**une chambre à un lit/deux lits**
What's the rate per night?	**Quel est le prix pour une nuit?**

AIRPORTS *(aéroport)*

Tunis-Carthage International Airport is 8 km (5 miles) northeast of Tunis city centre. Facilities include a duty-free shop, currency exchange, travel agencies, car-hire (car-rental) desks, restaurant, and coffee bar. Porters are available to help with luggage. Taxis can be picked up outside the terminal, and take about 15 minutes to reach the city centre.

Charter airlines fly into **Habib Bourguiba International Airport** at Skanès-Monastir (8km/5 miles west of Monastir). It too offers good facilities. Package tourists will be met by a coach; independent travellers can take the Metro (the station is just 100 metres/328 feet from the terminal) to Monastir or Sousse. Trains run hourly between 4am and 1am.

BICYCLE and MOPED HIRE
(location de bicyclettes/motos)

Bicycles and mopeds can be rented by the hour or day in Nabeul, Hammamet, and Houmt Souk. A cash deposit (or credit card) is required, and a valid licence for anything larger than 50cc. Inspect the bike carefully before taking it, and check that the quoted rates for mopeds and motorbikes include tax and insurance.

CAMPING *(le camping)*

To date, Tunisia has only a few official camping sites with electricity, water and shops. The most popular are at Hammam-Lif (20 km/12 miles east of Tunis), Hammamet, Nabeul, and Zarzis. Elsewhere you can camp almost anywhere, but use discretion and good sense, and always ask permission from the landowner, or from the local police. The O.N.T.T. (see TOURIST INFORMATION OFFICES) has current prices and information about the recognized camping sites.

CAR RENTAL *(location de voitures)* (See also DRIVING)

Renting a car is an ideal but expensive way of exploring Tunisia. There are numerous rental firms in the tourist resorts and main towns; local firms often charge less than the big international chains. Rates vary, and you should shop around—the best rates are usually found by booking and paying for a car before leaving home. Check that the quoted rate includes unlimited mileage, Collision Damage Waiver, Personal Accident Insurance, and Value Added Tax (T.V.A. in Tunisia).

Usually you must be over 21 to hire a car. You will need a full, valid driver's licence, held for at least 12 months, a passport, and a major credit card—cash deposits are prohibitively large.

CLIMATE and CLOTHING

Climate. Northern and central Tunisia enjoy a Mediterranean climate, with hot, dry summers and mild, rainy winters. The coastal resorts are hot and sunny from mid-May to mid-September, though at either end of the season the evenings can be a bit chilly. The hills of the north coast are the wettest part of the country. In winter, the weather can often be cold and grey in Tunis and the north.

The desert of southern Tunisia has little rainfall and summer temperatures of over 40°C (104°F). The sea tempers the coastal climate, and Djerba's maximum of around 30°C (86°F) is more comfortable.

The following chart shows the average daily maximum temperatures for each month in Tunis and Djerba, and the sea temperatures on Tunisian beaches:

		J	F	M	A	M	J	J	A	S	O	N	D
Tunis	°C	11	12	13	16	19	24	26	26	26	20	16	12
	°F	52	54	55	61	66	75	79	79	79	68	61	54
Djerba	°C	11	13	16	19	21	24	27	28	26	23	16	14
	°F	52	55	61	66	69	75	81	82	79	75	61	52
Sea temp	°C	14	13	14	16	18	21	24	26	26	24	17	11
	°F	57	55	57	61	64	69	75	79	79	75	63	52

Clothing. From June to September lightweight cottons are best, but remember a jacket or sweater for the evenings. Remember also a long-sleeved shirt and sun hat to protect against the strong midday sunshine. At other times a light jacket and a raincoat or umbrella will be handy, plus a warm coat for cool desert nights.

Respectable clothing should be worn if you are away from the beach or hotel, especially in mosques and other Islamic monuments—long trousers or skirt and long-sleeved shirt or blouse are best.

COMMUNICATIONS
(See also OPENING HOURS and TIME DIFFERENCES)

Post Offices. Post offices (*la poste*) are marked by a yellow sign with the letters "PTT." If you want stamps, go to the counter marked "*timbres*." Hours are generally Mon–Sat 8am–6pm (1

Tunisia

July–15 Sept); Mon–Sat 7:30am–1:30pm (16 Sept–30 June); and Sun 9-11am. During Ramadan hours are Mon–Sat 9am–1:30pm.

Main post offices maintain longer hours for the sale of stamps and for sending telegrams. In Tunis, Sfax, Houmt Souk, and Sousse these services are available 24 hours a day. Postage stamps can also be purchased at tobacconists' kiosks (*tabacs*) and hotel desks, and a tourist shops that sell postcards. Letters and cards to the U.K. take about four or five days to arrive.

Poste restante (general delivery). If you don't know ahead of time where you'll be staying, you can have your mail addressed to the post office in whichever town is most convenient, marked R.P. (for *Recette Postale*) and with your surname underlined, e.g.:

> Ms. Joan <u>Smith</u>
> Tunis R.P., Rue Charles de Gaulle
> Tunis
> Tunisia

It will be held for you at the main post office, and a small charge will be made. There can be confusion with the filing of European names —if you are expecting mail and there is nothing under your surname ask the staff to check under your first name, and even under "M" for Mr/Mrs/Miss/Ms. Take your passport along as identification.

Telephones. Domestic and international calls can be made from public telephones in the main post office, from *Taxiphone* agencies, or from call boxes on the street (*cabines*), which take 100M, 500M, and TD1 coins. To make a call within Tunisia, lift the receiver, insert your coins, and simply dial the number, including the two-digit area code for calls outside the city. The ringing tone is a single long tone (**NB** All five-digit numbers in Tunisia have recently been changed to six digits. If you dial the old number, a recorded message in French, English, and Arabic will tell you which number to add.)

To make an international call, dial 00 and wait for a second tone, then dial the country code (U.K.: 44; U.S.A. and Canada: 1), and the full number including area code, minus the initial zero. To make a re verse-charge (collect) call, dial the international operator and ask to be connected to an operator in your home country.

A stamp, please.	**Un timbre, s'il vous plaît.**
express (special delivery)	**par exprès**
airmail	**par avion**

COMPLAINTS

Complaints should first be made to the management of the establishment involved. If this doesn't work, request the complaints book (*livre des réclamations*); the law requires that all hotels, restaurants, and official guides provide one. Usually, just demanding it will settle the matter; if not, then seek advice from the local branch of the O.N.T.T. (see TOURIST INFORMATION OFFICES).

CRIME (See also EMERGENCIES and POLICE)

Tunisia has a moderate crime rate. The usual precautions should be taken: don't carry large amounts of cash; leave valuables in the hotel safe; and beware of pickpockets. Never leave bags or valuables on view in a parked car—take them with you or lock them in the boot (trunk). Any theft or loss must be reported immediately to the police in order to comply with your travel insurance. If your passport is lost or stolen, you should also inform your consulate.

In public, women should take care to dress conservatively and refrain from going out alone to avoid the possibility of harrassment.

CUSTOMS (*douane*) and ENTRY FORMALITIES

Citizens of the E.U., U.S.A., Canada, and Japan need only a passport and return ticket for visits of up to 90 days (a one-year British Visitor's Passport is also acceptable); the passport must be valid for a minimum of three months after the date you arrive.

You will have to fill in an immigration form before your flight lands: hand it over to the immigration officer, with your passport, on arrival.

Visas. Citizens of Australia and New Zealand must have a visa and return ticket to enter Tunisia. These must be applied for at least three weeks before the date of travel, at any Tunisian Embassy. (Visa regulations change from time to time, and should be checked with your travel agent.)

Duty-free allowance. The list that follows details duty-free allowances going into Tunisia, and, when returning, into your own country: **Tunisia:** 400 cigarettes or 100 cigars or 500*g* of tobacco, 2*l* of wine, and 1*l* of spirits; **U.S.A.:** 200 cigarettes or 50 cigars or 2*kg* tobacco, 1*l* of wine or spirits; **Australia:** 250 cigarettes or 250*g* tobacco, 1*l* alcohol; **Canada:** 200 cigarettes and 50 cigars and 400*g* tobacco, 1.1*l* wine or spirits or 8.5*l* beer; **New Zealand:** 200 cigarettes or 50 cigars or 250*g* tobacco, 4.5*l* wine or beer and 1.1*l* spirits; **Republic of Ireland:** 200 cigarettes or 50 cigars or 250*g* tobacco, 2*l* wine or 1*l* spirits; **South Africa:** 400 cigarettes and 50 cigars and 250*g* tobacco, 2*l* wine and 1*l* spirits; **U.K.:** 200 cigarettes or 50 cigars or 250*g* tobacco, 2*l* wine or 1*l* spirits.

Currency restrictions. You can take as much foreign currency as you like into or out of the country, but amounts in excess of 500 dinars equivalent must be declared on entry. The amount of dinars you can reconvert on departure must not exceed 30% of the total of all your exchange receipts, up to a maximum of 100 dinars. It is illegal to import or export Tunisian dinars.

I've nothing to declare.   **Je n'ai rien à déclarer**.
It's for my personal use.   **C'est pour mon usage personnel**

D

DRIVING (See also CAR HIRE)

Motorists planning to take their own vehicle into Tunisia will need a full driver's licence, an International Motor Insurance Certificate and "Green Card," and a Vehicle Registration Document. An official nationality plate must be displayed near the rear number plate, and head lamp beams must be adjusted for driving on the right. A red warning triangle must be carried. Motorcycle riders and their passengers must wear crash helmets. Note that the minimum legal age for driving in

Tunisia is 21 years old. Full details are available from the automobile associations or your insurance company.

Driving conditions. Drive on the right, pass on the left. Speed limits are 110 km/h (70 mph) on the motorway, 90 km/h (55 mph) on highways, and 50 km/h (30 mph) in towns and cities. Traffic joining a road from the right has priority, unless signs or markings indicate otherwise. Most importantly, this means that cars already in a roundabout must give way to those joining it (i.e., the opposite of what happens in most other countries). One local quirk you should be prepared for is that drivers making a left turn on a two-lane road often move over to the wrong side of the road before turning. This can be rather disconcerting if you are travelling in the opposite direction.

Driving conditions outside the cities are, on the whole, good on the main routes, with long, straight stretches, and little traffic. Minor roads are often wide enough for one vehicle only, and you will have to move onto the gravel shoulder to pass oncoming traffic. You should look out for pedestrians, donkey carts, and mopeds, especially near towns, where the former two often wander across the road without any apparent concern for their own safety. They also make driving after dark particularly hazardous.

If you plan to explore off the main routes, a reliable road map is essential. Many minor roads are unsurfaced, and should not be attempted without a four-wheel-drive vehicle and a local guide (rental cars do not carry insurance for unsurfaced roads). Many of the minor roads in the south can be rendered impassable by flash floods.

Petrol. Petrol (*essence*) and diesel (*gas-oil*) are easily obtained. There are plenty of service stations in and around towns, but they can be few and far between in the south, so always fill up at the beginning of the day when you are travelling in the more remote areas. Most cars take premium grade (*super*); lead-free gasoline (*sansplomb*) is available only in the larger towns.

Parking. Parking is rarely a problem, except in central Tunis, where illegally parked cars will be towed away. The best idea is to choose a hotel in Carthage or Sidi Bou Saïd where you can park, leave your car there, and take the Metro into the city centre.

Traffic police. Motorcycle police patrol the main highways, and occasionally set up checkpoints. You may be asked to produce your passport and registration or car-rental documents, but once the officer realises that you are a tourist, he will usually just wave you on. More often, a policeman will wave you down to ask for a lift either for himself or for a friend.

Breakdown. In most towns there should be no problem finding a mechanic for minor repairs. Larger towns and cities have full repair shops and towing services. If you break down in the more remote parts of the country, you will probably have to rely on assistance from passing cars, or carry out repairs yourself. If you have a rental car, follow the procedure set by the rental company—there will usually be a 24-hour emergency telephone number which you can call, and the company will arrange for either repairs or a replacement.

Anyone planning to travel off the main roads in the south of the country should be prepared: a four-wheel-drive vehicle, equipped for desert survival, is necessary, and you must inform the National Guard post in the nearest town of your proposed route and destination.

Road signs. Roads are generally well marked and virtually all directional signs are in both French and Arabic. Other signs are the familiar international pictographs. Listed below is a selection of of signs which you may come across in French, plus a number of words and phrases which you may find useful:

Attention	Caution
Attention travaux	caution, road works
Crue	Liable to flood during rains
Déviation	Diversion (detour)
Serrez à droite	Keep to the right
Défense de stationner	No parking
Virages	Bends (curves)

Other useful driving vocabulary:

(international) driving licence	**permis de conduire (international)**
car registration papers	**carte grise**
insurance certificate	**certificat d'assurance**
My car has broken down.	**Ma voiture est en panne.**
There's been an accident.	**Il y a eu un accident.**

E

ELECTRIC CURRENT

200V/50Hz AC is standard. An adapter for two-pin sockets will be needed; American 110V appliances will also require a transformer.

What's the voltage?	**Quel est le voltage?**
an adapter plug/a battery	**une prise de raccordement/ une pile**

EMBASSIES and CONSULATES

British Embassy	5 place de la Victoire, Tunis, tel. (01) 341444.
British Consulate	141–143 avenue de la Liberté, Tunis, tel. (01) 793322.
Canadian Embassy	3 rue de Sénégal, Tunis, tel. (01) 286557.
U.S. Embassy	144 avenue de la Liberté, Tunis, tel. (01) 782566.

EMERGENCIES (See also EMBASSIES and POLICE)

The national emergency telephone number is **197;** it helps if you are fluent in French or Arabic.

Police	**197**
Ambulance	**197**
Fire	**198**

Tunisia

ETIQUETTE

It is customary to shake hands on meeting, and then to place your right hand briefly over your heart. If you are invited into a Tunisian home, remember to remove your shoes before entering. Most important of all is dress: away from the beach, you should dress modestly, and avoid shorts and skimpy tops. Choose long trousers or a skirt reaching below the knee, with a long-sleeved top; women travelling alone will attract less attention if they wear a head scarf. (See also WOMEN TRAVELLERS.)

GUIDES and TOURS

If you are on a package tour, a guide will be provided when you visit Roman ruins or the medina in Tunis. The only place where official, English-speaking guides can be hired independently is at the tourist office in Kairouan (see TOURIST INFORMATION OFFICES).

A number of unofficial "guides" and hustlers often tout for business around the medina gates. They can be very persistent. If you genuinely don't want their services, be firm and polite, and don't lose your temper. If you do decide to engage one, make sure you agree in advance *exactly* what you want to see, and the price to be paid (generally about half the cost of an official guide). They will invariably try to take you to a shop, under various pretexts, since they can earn commission from the owner. If you don't want to buy anything, then politely insist on not going in.

LANGUAGE

The official language of Tunisia is Arabic, but a large proportion of the population is bilingual in Arabic and French; most signs and street names are in both languages also. Although written Arabic is the same throughout the Arab world, the spoken dialect of Tunisian Arabic is quite distinctive, and travellers who have learned the Arabic of the Middle East will struggle to get by. In the main destinations many people speak some English, and almost all speak French.

Although Tunisians will always greet you in French or English, it is polite to learn a few basic phrases—local people will welcome any attempt you make:

Good morning	**S'báh 'l khéy**
You're welcome	**Áfwen**
Good night	**Tis 'báh "l khéyr**
Good afternoon	**Msá 'l khéyr**
Goodbye	**Beslémeh**
Please	**Min fádlak**
Thank you	**Bárakallahúfik, shókran**

Some useful expressions in French:

you're welcome	**je vous en prie**
where/when/how	**où/quand/comment**
yesterday/today/tomorrow	**hier/aujourd'hui/demain**
day/week/month/year	**jour/semaine/mois/année**
left/right	**gauche/droite**
big/small	**grand/petit**
cheap/expensive	**bon marché/cher**
open/closed	**ouvert/fermé**
here/there	**ici/là**
Does anyone here speak English?	**Y a-t-il quelqu'un ici qui parle anglais?**
What does this mean?	**Que signifie ceci?**
Get a doctor, quickly!	**Un médecin, vite!**

LAUNDRY *(blanchissage)*

Even a modest one-star establishment will have a laundry service. Washing should be handed in before noon for return the following morning. There are no coin-operated self-service launderettes.

LOST PROPERTY *(trouvés)*

Ask for advice from your hotel receptionist or the local Tourist Information Office before contacting the police. For items left behind on public transport, ask your hotel receptionist to telephone the bus or train station or taxi company. (See also CRIME.)

I've lost my handbag/ wallet/passport.	**J'ai perdu mon sac à main/portefeuille/passeport.**

M

MEDIA

Radio. If you have a short-wave radio you will be able to pick up the BBC World Service and Voice of America. Otherwise, you can listen to local stations which offer a choice of traditional and pop music, or news, sport, and current affairs in French or Arabic.

Television. You will find a TV supplied in the more expensive hotels; there are two relayed foreign channels, France 2 and Rai Uno, and one local channel. The better hotels also have satellite TV with the French channel TV5, and Sky, CNN, MTV, and Superchannel.

Newspapers. Local French-language papers include *La Presse, L'Action,* and *Le Temps*, all of which provide a rather thin diet of North African and international news and sports. The French dailies *Le Monde* and *Le Figaro*, and the American *International Herald Tribune* are also widely available on city news-stands. British newspapers can be found, a day or two after publication, on city centre newsstands in Tunis, and in the coastal resorts.

Have you any English-language newspapers/magazines?	**Avez-vous des journaux/ revues en anglais?**

MEDICAL CARE (See also EMERGENCIES)

There is no free health care for visitors to Tunisia—all medical services must be paid for. You should not leave home without adequate insurance, preferably including cover for an emergency flight home.

in the event of serious injury or illness. Your travel agent, bank, building society, or insurance broker can provide a comprehensive policy which will cover not only medical costs, but also theft or loss of money and possessions, delayed or cancelled flights, and so on.

Health hazards. The main health hazards in Tunisia are stomach upsets and sunburn. Take a sun hat, sunglasses, and plenty of high-factor sunscreen, and limit your sunbathing sessions to an hour or less until you begin to tan. Sunburn can seriously ruin your holiday.

Diarrhoea can be avoided by eating only freshly cooked food, and drinking only bottled water and canned or bottled drinks (without ice). Avoid restaurants that look dirty, food from street stalls, undercooked meat, salads and fruit (except fruit you can peel yourself, such as bananas, oranges, melons, etc.), dairy products, and tap water. The standards of hygiene in most tourist hotels and restaurants are usually adequate, but you can never be sure.

If you are unfortunate enough to catch a stomach bug, rest and take plenty of fluids to avoid dehydration—soft drinks will do, but a solution of four heaped teaspoons of sugar and a half teaspoon of salt in a litre (quart) of bottled water is best. Most cases go in three or four days; if symptoms persist, seek medical advice.

Chemists/drugstores. For minor ailments, ask advice from the local pharmacy (*pharmacie*). These are usually open during normal shopping hours. After hours, at least one per town remains open all night, called the *pharmacie de service* or *pharmacie de nuit*; its location is posted in the windows of all other pharmacies.

Vaccinations. There are no compulsory immunisation requirements for entry into Tunisia, but inoculations against tetanus, polio, typhoid, and hepatitis A are recommended.

MONEY MATTERS

Currency (*monnaie*). The unit of currency is the Tunisian dinar (D), divided into 1,000 millimes (M). Notes come in denominations of 5D, 10D, and 20D (rare), and coins in 10, 20, 50, 100M, ½D, and 1D.

Tunisia

The dinar is a soft currency, and the exchange rate is controlled by the government, so there's no point shopping around for the best rate —they're all the same. (See also CUSTOMS & ENTRY FORMALITIES.)

Banks and currency exchange (*banque*; *change*). Nothing about opening hours is sure, but between October 1 and July 1, banks normally open Mon–Thurs 8–11am, 2–4pm Fri 8–11am, 1–3pm; during Ramadan hours are 8–11am and 1–2:30pm; and in summer 7:30 or 8–11am or noon only. The most efficient service is usually the S.T.B. (*Société Tunisianne de Banque*). The normal procedure is for the clerk to fill out the forms at the counter, then give you a receipt or token which you take to the cashier (*la caisse*) where you pick up your cash. Since this involves queuing twice, changing money can be a time-consuming business. In popular resorts like Monastir, some banks and exchange booths open longer, often 8am–8pm including weekends. Airport exchange desks are open 24 hours, but may close between flight arrivals. Most hotels, 3 stars and above, exchange money as well.

Traveller's cheques (*chèques de voyages*). These are accepted by most banks and hotels, though smaller establishments may refuse to cash them and will direct you elsewhere; Thomas Cook and American Express are the most widely accepted. You will need your passport, and occasionally the purchase receipts too; no commission is charged. You can exchange cash easily in hotels and tourist shops.

Credit cards (*cartes de crédit*). Major credit and charge cards— Visa, Access/Mastercard, American Express, and Diners Club— are accepted in the more expensive hotels (three-star and up) and restaurants in the larger cities, and by tourist shops and car rental firms. If you are unsure whether an establishment will accept your card, ask first. Visa and Access/Mastercard can also be used in large branches of banks to obtain cash advances, though this can take time.

PLANNING YOUR BUDGET

To give you an idea of what to expect, here's a list of prices in Tunisian dinars (DT) and millimes (M). These can only be regarded as approximate, as inflation continues to push costs up.

Airport transfer. Taxi, Tunis Airport to city centre, 2DT (5DT at night); bus, 500M. Metro, Monastir Airport to Monastir, 700M.

Bicycle and moped hire. Bicycles 1DT/hour, 6DT/day. Mopeds 4DT/hour, 18DT/day.

Buses. Tunis city buses charge a flat fare of 350M. Inter-city coaches from Tunis to Sousse cost 2.500DT; Tunis to Tabarka 3.500DT; Tunis to Kairouan 3.450DT.

Camping. In official sites, around 2DT per person per night, plus 2DT for a car, and 1DT for a caravan.

Car hire. Renault Super 5—30DT plus 290M per km for 1 day, and 550DT for 7 days (unlimited km). Petrol costs 570M per litre.

Excursions. Day trip from Hammamet to Tunis, Carthage, and Sidi Bou Saïd, 22DT. Three-day Land Rover "safari" around southern Tunisia from Sousse, 80DT.

Ferries. Car ferry from Jorf to Djerba, 600M per car; from Sfax to Kerkennah Isles, 3.5 DT.

Hotels (double room with bath and breakfast, in summer). 1-star 18DT; 2-star 30DT; 3-star 50DT; 4-star 75DT; 4-star Luxe 100DT and up.

Meals and drinks. Coffee 500M–1DT; soft drinks 500M–1DT; beer 1.500–2DT; bottle of mineral water 1DT. Meals, per head, incl. drink: lunch in café, 5–10DT; lunch in waterfront restaurant, 25DT; dinner in hotel, 15-20DT; dinner in good restaurant, 30+DT.

Metro. Tunis city centre to the Bardo Museum, 700M. The T.G.M. train from the city centre to Sidi Bou Saïd costs 500M one way.

Sightseeing. Admission to most museums and archaeological sites is 1DT; the Bardo, Carthage, El Djem, and Kairouan cost 2DT. There is a 1DT surcharge for camera or video.

Tunisia

Taxis. The fare for a cross-town trip in Tunis is 1.500 to 2DT.

Trains. From Tunis to Sousse, first class, 7.150DT; Sousse to Gabès, first class, 11.750 DT. The *Lézard Rouge* tourist train costs 9.500DT round trip from Metlaoui.

O

OPENING HOURS (*heures d'ouverture*)

Archaeological sites. 8am to 6pm daily.

Banks. 1 Oct–1 July, Mon–Fri 8–11am, 2–4pm; rest of the year 7:30 or 8–11am or noon only; during Ramadan 8–11 am, 1–2:30pm.

Currency exchange offices. 8am–8pm daily in popular resorts.

Museums. Bardo 9am–5pm (summer), 9:30am–4:30pm (winter), closed Mon, holidays; Carthage 8am–7pm (summer), 8:30am–5:30pm (winter) daily; Sousse Archaeological 8am–noon, 3–7pm summer (9am–noon, 2–6pm winter) daily.

Post office. 1 July–15 Sept, Mon–Sat 8am–6pm; 16 Sept–30 June, Mon–Sat 7:30am–1:30pm; and Sun 9–11am. During Ramadan, Mon–Sat 9am–1:30pm.

Shops. Generally 8:00am–12:30pm and 2:30–6:00pm; some close for short periods on Fridays, the Muslim holy day.

P

PHOTOGRAPHY (*la photographie*)

Film is widely available, but can be expensive. Shops in major resorts process colour prints in 24 to 48 hours at reasonable prices, and some offer a 1-hour service. The use of flash or tripod is forbidden in some museums, so always check. Most museums and archaeological sites charge an extra fee for the use of a camera or video.

Away from the resorts, if you want to take photos of local people, ask first—many country people object to having their picture taken.

I'd like a film.	**J'aimerais un film.**
a black-and-white film	**un film noir et blanc**

a film for colour prints	**un film couleurs**
a colour-slide film	**un film pour diapositives**
Can I take a picture?	**Puis-je prendre une photo?**

POLICE *(la police)* (See also EMERGENCIES)

Tunisia's civil police *(Sûreté Nationale)* wear blue-grey uniforms. There is a police station *(poste de police* or *gendarmerie)* in most towns. If you want to report a crime, it is a good idea to get a fluent French or Arabic speaker to help you—your hotel or the local tourist office may assist. In an emergency, dial 197. The *Sûreté* also man traffic checkpoints and patrol the highways (see DRIVING).

| I want to report a theft. | **Je veux signaler un vol.** |
| My ticket/wallet/passport has been stolen. | **On a volé mon billet/porte-feuille/passeport.** |

PUBLIC HOLIDAYS *(jours feriés)*

Tunisia has two kinds of public holiday: secular holidays (same date each year), and religious holidays (which fall according to the lunar calendar). Many businesses close on the following secular holidays:

1 January	*Jour de l'An*	New Year's Day
20 March	*Fête de l'Indépendance*	Independence Day
21 March	*Fête de la Jeunesse*	Youth Day
9 April	*Anniversaire Martyrs des*	Martyrs' Day
1 May	*Fête du Travail*	Labour Day
25 July	*Fête de la République*	Republic day
13 August	*Fête de la Femme*	Women's Day
15 October	*Fête de l'Evacuation*	
7 November	*Fête de la Nouvelle Epoque*	New Era Day (Anniversary of the Events of 1987)

The religious holidays listed below are marked by two days off. Public transport may be reduced. The dates, which are determined by sightings of the moon, are often announced only days before the holiday, so check with your travel agent or the Tunisian Embassy to ascertain actual dates:

February or March	*Aïd es-Seghir*	"Little Feast," the end of the month of Ramadan
April or May	*Aïd el-Kebir*	"Great Feast," commemorating the sacrifice of Abraham
June or July	*Moharem*	Muslim New Year
August	*Mouloud*	Birthday of the Prophet Mohammed

Ramadan falls the four weeks before Aïd es-Seghir, during which many businesses adopt special opening hours, closing at dusk as workers head home to break their fast. (See also FESTIVALS).

R

RELIGION

Tunisia is Muslim, but is very tolerant of other faiths. Christians account for only 0.1% of the population, but there are Roman Catholic churches in most large towns and tourist resorts, and Anglican and Protestant churches in Tunis. Jewish synagogues can be found in Tunis and Djerba. Details of local religious services are held by the local tourist office (see TOURIST INFORMATION OFFICES).

T

TIME DIFFERENCES

Tunisia runs one hour ahead of G.M.T. all year round, making it the same time as the U.K. in summer, and one hour ahead in winter. The table below shows the time difference in various cities in summer.

New York	London	**Tunisia**	Sydney	Los Angeles
6am	11am	**noon**	9pm	3am

TIPPING *(pourboires)*

It is customary to offer a tip for services rendered. 100 millimes is usual for café waiters, porters, petrol pump attendants, and guardians at monuments and museums; restaurant waiters expect 10–15% or 500M per person on top of any service charge. If a taxi driver uses his meter, then tip 10–15% of the fare; if you agree a price beforehand, nothing extra will be expected.

TOILETS/RESTROOMS *(toilettes; W.C.)*

Public toilets are few and far between outside airports and major railway stations; if you need one in a hurry, try a café or restaurant.

TOURIST INFORMATION OFFICES
(office de tourisme; syndicat d'initiative)

The Tunisian National Tourist Office (*Organisation Nationale de Tourisme Tunisian*, or O.N.T.T.) has a head office in Tunis (see below), and branches in towns and resorts throughout the country. The staff can help with general inquiries, advise on local accommodation (no booking service), and provide maps and brochures.

Tunis	Head office, 1 avenue Mohamed V, tel. (01) 341077.
Djerba	avenue Habib Bourguiba, tel. (05) 650016.
Hammamet	avenue Habib Bourguiba, tel. (02) 280423.
Kairouan	place du Commandant Mohamed el Befaoui, tel. (07) 220452.
Monastir	Airport, tel. (03) 4630216.
Nabeul	avenue Taieb M'Hiri, tel. (02) 286737.
Skanès	Quartier Chraka (near Hotels Metro Station), tel. (03) 461205.
Sousse	1 avenue Habib Bourguiba, tel. (03) 425157.
Tozeur	avenue Abou el Kacem Chebbi, tel. (06) 250503.

Tunisia

Opening hours are generally Mon–Thurs 8:30am–1pm, 3–5:45pm, Fri–Sat 8:30am–1:30pm (7:30am–1:30pm Jul/Aug), closed Sun. Most towns also have a *Syndicat d'Initiative*, a local information office.

The O.N.T.T. maintains a number of overseas offices, from which you can obtain information prior to booking your holiday.

Canada   Tourist Section, Tunisian Embassy, 515 Oscannor Street, Ottawa, tel. (613) 237-0330.

U.K.   77A Wigmore Street, London W1H 9LJ, tel. (0171) 224 5561.

U.S.A.   Tourist Section, Tunisian Embassy, 1515 Massachusetts Avenue NW, Washington D.C. 20005, tel. (202) 862-1850.

TRANSPORT

Buses. Tunisia is covered by a comprehensive bus network. Inter-city coaches run by S.N.T.R.I. (*Société Nationale de Transport Rural et Interurbain*) link Tunis with every major town in the country; regional companies link the major towns with villages in the surrounding area. Tickets are cheap and can be bought at the bus station before departure. Timetable information is hard to find; try the local O.N.T.T. office or *Syndicat d'Initiative*, or ask a driver—destinations are written in French as well as Arabic. Popular routes, with approximate journey times, are: Tunis–Sousse, 2 hours 15 minutes; Tunis–Kairouan, 4 hours; Tunis–Tabarka, 4 hours; Sousse–Sfax, 2 hours 30 minutes; Sfax–Tozeur, 5 hours 30 minutes.

Tunis has good city buses, and maps are posted in the terminals.

When's the next bus to...?	**Quand part le prochain bus pour...?**
single (one-way)	**un aller simple**
return (round trip)	**un aller-retour**

Ferries. There are two car-ferry services: Jorf to Ajim on the island of Djerba, departing every 30 minutes, crossing time 15 minutes; and

Sfax to the Kerkennah Islands, four crossings a day, journey time 1 hour 15 minutes.

Louages. A faster and slightly more comfortable alternative to the bus for shorter journeys between towns is the *louage*. This is a large estate car seating six passengers, which shuttles back and forth along a set route. There are no fixed departure times; the taxi departs as soon as all the seats are full. To find a seat, you simply turn up at the "terminal," usually a piece of waste ground on the edge of the town centre (the tourist office or your hotel will tell you where—there's usually a different location for different destinations), and ask the drivers. Fares are per person for a full car; ask other passengers (or your hotel receptionist) what the standard fare is.

Metro. Tunis's light rail network is the Metro. The most useful line is Line 4, linking place Barcelone in the centre (via Line 2, change at République) with the Bardo Museum. The Metro is linked (via Tunis Marine station at the foot of avenue Habib Bourguiba) with another railway, the TGM (Tunis–Goulette-Marsa), which runs every 15 minutes to Carthage, Sidi Bou Saïd and La Marsa.

Another Metro service links Monastir and Sousse, with stops at Monastir International Airport, and the Skanès hotel zone. Trains run hourly from 7am to 8pm.

Taxis. See also LOUAGES, above. Taxis can be hailed in the street, or picked up at a rank. Meters are used, and rates are low by European standards. All taxis levy a 50% surcharge for night travel (usually 10pm–6am April–Sept, 9pm–7am Oct–March), when you will probably have to negotiate a price, especially from the airport.

What's the fare to...? **Quel est le tarif pour...?**

Trains. The national rail company, S.N.C.F.T. (*Société Nationale des Chemins de Fer Tunisiens*), maintains a limited but efficient rail network from Tunis north to Tabarka and south to Nabeul, Sousse, Sfax, Gabès, Gafsa, and Tozeur. Mainline trains are comfortable and inexpensive (slightly slower but more comfortable than the bus). There are three classes: *grand confort* (luxury), first class, and second class. Full timetables (*horaires*) are posted in main stations; buy tickets a day in advance (or you may have to pay double the fare; round-trip tickets are cheaper)for a seat in an air-conditioned carriage (*voiture grand confort*). From Tunis to Sousse takes about 3 hours, to Gabès, 7 hours.

A special tourist train called the *Lézard Rouge* (Red Lizard) runs from Metlaoui through the spectacular Seldja Gorge, hauling restored 19th-century carriages (see page 67).

TRAVELLERS with DISABILITIES

As yet there are very few facilities for disabled travellers in Tunisia. Getting around the city centres, especially the medinas, in a wheelchair is difficult, and most public transport is inaccessible. Some of the more modern beach hotels, however, do have wheelchair access. Make enquiries through a tour operator, stating your exact needs, before booking. While in Tunisia, the national organisation for the disabled, A.G.I.M. (*Association Générale des Insuffisants Moteurs*) may be able to help with specific enquiries, tel. (01) 520365.

TRAVELLING to TUNISIA

By Air

Scheduled flights

From the U.K. and Ireland: The national airline, Tunis Air, flies from London Heathrow to Tunis three times a week, with connecting services to Monastir-Skanès, Sfax, Djerba, and Nefta-Tozeur. For details call your local Tunis Air office or representative. GB Airways flies three times a week from London Gatwick to Tunis. For details, contact British Airways. There are no direct flights from Ireland.

From the U.S.A. and Canada: There are no direct flights from North America to Tunisia; you will have to fly via London, Paris, Amsterdam, or Rome.

Charter flights and package tours

From the U.K. and Ireland: U.K. charter flights are available from Gatwick, Birmingham, Manchester, and Glasgow to Monastir. Charter flights from Ireland operate during the summer. These are either flight only (cheaper than a scheduled flight, but with more restrictions), or as part of a hotel or self-catering package holiday. Most companies offer a variety of excursions. An increasingly popular option is the adventure holiday, which combines a week in a coastal resort with a week-long Land Rover safari to the desert oases, Matmata, and *ksour* villages of the south. For full details ask a travel agent.

By Road and Sea

The main route from the French ferry ports runs south to Geneva and through the Mont Blanc Tunnel to the Italian ports of Genoa, and Tràpani in Sicily, which have car-ferry services to Tunis. The latter is faster and cheaper, with a shorter sea crossing (10 hours). Tickets must be bought at least three months in advance for a summer crossing.

A car ferry also runs from Marseille to Tunis (crossing time 24 hours). For details, contact a travel agent.

A hydrofoil operates during the summer season from Tràpani to Kélibia (3 hours).

WATER

Although the tap water is said to be safe in most parts of Tunisia, you are recommended to avoid it. Bottled mineral water is easily bought —*Safia* and *Aïn Oktor* (still) are the most popular brands; the latter has a strong mineral flavour. *Aïn Garci* is carbonated.

WEIGHTS and MEASURES (See also DRIVING)

Tunisia uses the metric system.

WOMEN TRAVELLERS

It is unfortunate, but true, that foreign women travelling in Tunisia are often subject to harassment from local men. This can range from catcalls and whistles to rude comments and bottom-pinching. A woman accompanied by a man is less likely to attract unwanted attention, but is not immune.

The way you dress is all-important; shorts and a halter top are not a good idea (although this does not apply to resorts such as Hammamet and Monastir, where beachwear is the norm, nor to downtown Tunis, where Tunisian women dress in European fashions). The best strategy is to dress modestly, in long trousers, or preferably a long skirt, and a long-sleeved, loose-fitting top.

Avoid eye contact with local men and ignore any rude comments. Try not to lose your temper, and don't get into an argument: it's highly likely that you will not get the better of your antagoniser, and you will probably get little in the way of sympathy from passersby.

Having said this, the majority of Tunisians are courteous and friendly, and will show you genuine hospitality. You just have to keep your wits about you and judge each encounter as it comes.

Y

YOUTH HOSTELS *(auberge de jeunesse)*

Tunisia has two dozen or so basic youth hostels and youth centres *(Maisons des Jeunes)*. You'll find the best ones are in Tunis, Aïn Draham, Gabès, and Houmt Souk. If you're planning to make use of youth hostels during your stay, contact your national youth hostel association before departure to obtain an international membership card. Further information and a full list of hostels in Tunisia (and worldwide) are available from the International Youth Hostel Federation (IYHF), 9 Guessens Road, Welwyn Garden City, Herts AL8 6QW, United Kingdom, tel. (01707) 324 170, fax (01707) 323 980.

Recommended Hotels

Our selection of hotels is based on the requirements of both group visitors and independent travellers, concentrating on locations that make useful base-camps or stop-overs during a tour of Tunisia. If you're travelling independently, most establishments are signposted from the main road.

The official star-rating of each hotel (see page 105) is given after its name ("u/c" means "unclassified"). As a basic guide, the symbols below indicate prices for a double room with bath, including breakfast, in high season:

✹✹✹✹	over 50 DT
✹✹✹	30–50 DT
✹✹	20–30 DT
✹	below 20 DT

BIZERTE

Continental (u/c) ✹ *29, rue du 2 Mars 1934; Tel. (02) 431436.* Cheap and cheerful, in the centre of Bizerte's ville nouvelle.

Petit Mousse (**) ✹✹ *Route de la Corniche; Tel. (02) 432185.* Small, friendly, family-run hotel overlooking the beach, with an excellent restaurant (see page 133). All rooms have a balcony with a sea view. Booking recommended.

CAP BON

Bellevue (**) ✹✹-✹✹✹ *Avenue Assad ibn el Fourat, Hammamet; Tel. (02) 281121.* Attractive, modern hotel east of town; most rooms have balconies with sea views. Can be noisy.

Sahbi (**) ✹✹ *Avenue de la République, Hammamet;* Tel. (02) 280807. Large, bright rooms—ask for one opening onto the terrace. Convenient location. Booking advised.

DJERBA

Arischa (*) ✾ *36, rue Ghazi Mustapha, Houmt Souk; Tel. (05) 650384.* An old *fondouk* (hostel for travelling merchants), complete with an attractive vine-draped courtyard, and a well where camels once quenched their thirst. Lively bar.

Marhala (u/c) ✾ *Rue Moncef Bey, Houmt Souk; Tel. (05) 650146.* Another old *fondouk,* converted by the *Touring Club de Tunisie* into a basic hotel full of character. Rooms are set around an attractive courtyard. Shared bathroom facilities.

Tanit (**) ✾✾✾-✾✾✾✾ *Ras Taguerness; Tel. (05) 657132.* Family-oriented hotel in a quiet location at the far eastern tip of the island. Comfy rooms in low-rise blocks, near restaurant, beach, and pool. Full watersports facilities.

DOUGGA

Thugga (**) ✾✾ *Route de Tunis, Tebboursouk; Tel. (08) 665713.* Comfortable and modern. Rooms on the old courtyard have traditional barrel-vaulted ceilings.

KAIROUAN

Continental (****) ✾✾✾ *Avenue el Moizz ibn Badis; Tel. (07) 221135.* Kairouan's biggest, smartest hotel, popular with groups. Good pool, and handy for the tourist office.

Splendid (***) ✾✾ *Rue du 9 Avril; Tel. (07) 220041.* Grand hotel with tiled decoration and airy rooms. Good restaurant.

Tunisia (**) ✾-✾✾ *Avenue Farhat Hached; Tel. (07) 221855.* Basic comfortable rooms with private bathrooms. No restaurant.

MATMATA

Marhala (u/c) ✾ *Tel. (05) 630015.* An underground hotel. Rooms are tiny and basic, facilities shared; bar and restaurant.

Matmata (**) ✾✾ *Tel. (05) 230066.* An average hotel with café, restaurant, pool, and comfortable rooms.

METAMEUR (NEAR MEDENINE)

Les Ghorfas (u/c) ✲ *Tel. (05) 640294.* Attractive hotel, once the village *ksar.* Rooms are small and basic, but comfortable. The owner organizes trips to nearby *ksar* villages.

MONASTIR

Festival (****) ✲✲✲✲ *Skanes-Monastir; Tel. (03) 467555.* Plush hotel near the airport (but not on the flight path). Attentive staff, fine food, and large rooms.

Monastir Beach Hotel ✲ *Monastir Beach; Tel. (03) 464766.* Clean, very basic rooms with great views of the beach and ocean.

Regency (****L) ✲✲✲✲ *Port de Plaisance; Tel. (03) 460033.* Monastir's top hotel: sumptuous rooms overlook the marina below the *ribat.* Expensive in summer, but check low-season rates.

SOUSSE

Kanta (****) ✲✲ *Port el Kantaoui; Tel. (03) 240466.* Luxury hotel in attractive gardens 8 km (5 miles) north of Sousse. Good health facilities, satellite TV.

Marabout (***) ✲✲✲-✲✲✲✲ *Boulevard 7 Novembre; Tel. (03) 226245.* A friendly, family-run hotel, mainly frequented by package tourists in high season. All rooms have a balcony and private bathroom. Swimming pool and tennis courts.

Sousse Azur (**) ✲✲✲ *Rue Amilcar; Tel. (03) 227760.* Small, friendly hotel off avenue Bourguiba in town centre. Bright rooms with private bathrooms.

TABARKA

De France (*) ✲-✲✲ *Avenue Bourguiba; Tel. (08) 644577.* Old-fashioned, comfortable, with a pleasant garden bar. Bourguiba stayed here during a period of exile from Tunis in 1952.

Hammam Bourguiba (***) ✲✲✲ *Hammam Bourguiba, near Aïn Draham.; Tel. (08) 632517.* Old-fashioned spa hotel built at a hot spring in the hills south of Tabarka, with mineral pools and massage rooms. Feels more like a clinic than a hotel, but makes an interesting change from the beach.

Les Mimosas (***) ❁❁❁❁ *Tel. (08) 643018.* Large, comfy rooms with *en suite* bathrooms. Pool and terrace garden on hillside. Approached by a private driveway on the left just after the turn off to Aïn Draham.

TOZEUR

Grand Oasis (***) ❁❁❁❁ *Place des Martyrs; Tel. (06) 452300/452699.* Large, attractive hotel on edge of palmery, with swimming pool and air-conditioning. Rooms decorated in traditional green (for palm leaves) and yellow (for the dates).

Splendid (*) ❁-❁❁ *Rue de Kairouan, Medina; Tel. (06) 450053.* Pleasant old-fashioned rooms surrounding a palm-shaded courtyard. Small swimming pool.

TUNIS

Africa Meridien (****Luxe) ❁❁❁❁ *50 avenue Bourguiba ; Tel. (01) 347477.* The only high-rise building in central Tunis. Luxurious rooms and facilities—even a private cinema.

Majestic (***) ❁❁❁ *36, avenue de Paris; Tel. (01) 332666.* Fine old building with French colonial "wedding cake" architecture, a bit worn around the edges.

Maison Dorée (**) ❁❁ *3, rue el Koufa; Tel. (01) 240631/2.* Clean and comfortable, pleasantly old-fashioned. Good restaurant.

Résidence Carthage (**) ❁❁❁ *16, rue Hannibal, Carthage;* Tel. (01) 731072. Family-run hotel with pleasant rooms and restaurant, close to the Carthage-Salammbo station.

Sidi Bou Said (****) ❁❁❁❁ *Avenue Sidi Dhrif, Sidi Bou Saïd; Tel. (01) 740411.* Stylish luxury hotel on a hilltop above the sea. Most rooms have wonderful views. Swimming pool.

Recommended Restaurants

In the main tourist resorts there is often little to distinguish between restaurants apart from price; most have similar menus offering one or two Tunisian dishes and French and/or Italian dishes. Generally, the farther away from the beach, main square, or main avenue a restaurant is located, the cheaper it will be. Expense doesn't necessarily mean quality—usually it means better location and flashier decor. You can eat well for very little money if you go off the beaten track, especially in the medina.

Below is a list of restaurants recommended by Berlitz. Reservations are not usually necessary, but where a booking might be appropriate, we have included the restaurant's telephone number. As a basic guide, the following symbols indicate the price of a three-course meal for two, excluding drinks:

✱✱✱	over 40 DT
✱✱	20–40 DT
✱	below 20 DT

BIZERTE
Le Petit Mousse ✱✱ *Route de la Corniche; Tel. (02) 432185.* Excellent value seafood restaurant, with dining room and terrace. Dinner bookings recommended.

CAP BON

Restaurant des Grottes ✱✱-✱✱✱ *El Haouaria.* Great situation on clifftop at end of road leading to caves (*grottes*), with view across sea to the islands of Zembra and Zembretta. Good fish and seafood, but rather pricey.

Restaurant de la Poste ✱✱ *Hammamet.* Opposite the medina entrance in the main square. Traditional Tunisian fare and a nice roof terrace.

La Pergola ✱✱✱ *Shopping Centre, Hammamet; Tel. (02) 280993.* One of Hammamet's top restaurants, chic and stylish, with a French/Tunisian menu.

DJERBA

Princesse d'Haroun ✱✱-✱✱✱ *Harbour, Houmt Souk; Tel. (05) 658561.* One of the best restaurants on the island, especially noted for its seafood. If you want to sample fresh lobster, octopus, and squid, then this is the place to come. Bookings recommended.

Du Sud ✱✱ *Place Hedi Chaker, Houmt Souk.* Pleasant restaurant located in the town centre; offers a good selection of Tunisian dishes and seafood, including an excellent *brik aux fruits de mer.*

KAIROUAN

Roi de Couscous ✱-✱✱ *Avenue du 20 Mars; Tel. (07) 221237.* One of the best places in Kairouan to try a classic Tunisian dinner of *chorba, brik, maqroudh,* and couscous. Reservations recommended.

Sabra ✱ *Avenue de la République; Tel. (07) 220260.* Popular and cheap little restaurant with friendly service, a good place if you're on a tight budget; come and fill up on couscous for a few dinars.

MATMATA

Hotel Matmata ✱✱ *Tel. (05) 230066.* This is the only real restaurant in the village, and is consequently often packed with tour groups at lunchtime. Serves classic Tunisian dishes. Poolside café-bar.

MONASTIR

Le Grill ✱✱✱ *Marina Cap Monastir; Tel. (03) 462136.* On the marina, serving mixed French and Tunisian cuisine. Very good.

SOUSSE

L'Escargot ❋❋-❋❋❋ *Route de la Corniche; Tel. (03) 224525.* The top restaurant in Sousse, offering quality French cuisine in chic, stylish surroundings. Bookings recommended.

Bonheur ❋❋ *Place Farhat Hached; Tel. (03) 225742.* One of the best of the many restaurants in the town centre, offering a selection of tasty European and Tunisian dishes.

TOZEUR

Le Petit Prince ❋❋ *In the Palmery.* This popular establishment, occupies a lovely spot amidst the date palms, 1 km (half a mile) from the town centre. Traditional Tunisian cuisine.

Le Pirate ❋ *Avenue Bourguiba.* A popular no-frills restaurant serving large helpings of couscous at rock-bottom prices.

TUNIS

M'rabet ❋❋❋ *Souk et Trouk, Medina; Tel. (01) 263681.* This well-known tourist restaurant near the Great Mosque is located in a fine old house which has been built over the tombs of three holy men. The mixed French/Tunisian menu is accompanied by a floor show with belly dancer.

Chez Nous ❋❋ *5, rue de Marseille; Tel. (01) 243048.* This is a stylish French restaurant serving worthwhile cuisine at very reasonable prices. Long a popular haunt, the walls are decorated with photos of famous customers.

Monte Carlo ❋❋ *Avenue Franklin Roosevelt, La Goulette; Tel. (01) 735338.* One of several good fish restaurants situated behind the harbour at La Goulette (easily accessible by TGM train). The freshly-caught fish are sold according to their weight.

Le Pirate ❋❋-❋❋❋ *Avenue du Pres. Kennedy; Tel. (01) 748266.* A sophisticated seafood restaurant located next to the marina at the foot of the cliff. You can reach it by taking the long flight of steps which lead down opposite the Hotel Dar Saïd.

ABOUT BERLITZ

In 1878 Professor Maximilian Berlitz had a revolutionary idea about making language learning accessible and enjoyable. One hundred and twenty years later these same principles are still successfully at work.

For language instruction, translation and interpretation services, cross-cultural training, study abroad programs, and an array of publishing products and additional services, visit any one of our more than 350 Berlitz Centers in over 40 countries.

Please consult your local telephone directory for the Berlitz Center nearest you or visit our web site at http://www.berlitz.com.

Helping the World Communicate